THE PROPH
MUHAMMAD ﷺ
FOR CHILDREN

By

Ameena Golding
Haya Hassan
Hibah Hassan
Sarah Ali
Umema Imran
Zineb Sarah Messaoui

Edited by

Tajwar Hassan

Goodword

Contents

Project editor: Vinni Rahman
Art editor: Mateen Ahmad
Graphic design: Pradeepan Kundathil
Illustrator: Gurmeet

First Published 2015

Goodword Books
A-21, Sector 4, Noida-201301, India
Tel. +91-8588822672, +91120-4314871
email: info@goodwordbooks.com
www.goodwordbooks.com

Goodword Books, Chennai
Tel. +9144-4352-4599
Mob. +91-9790853944, 9600105558
email: chennaigoodword@gmail.com

Islamic Vision Ltd.
426-434 Coventry Road, Small Heath
Birmingham B10 0UG, U.K.
Tel. 121-773-0137, Fax: 121-766-8577
e-mail: info@ipci-iv.co.uk
www.islamicvision.co.uk

Goodword Books, Hyderabad
Tel. 04023000131, Mob. 07032641415
email: hyd.goodword@gmail.com

IB Publisher Inc.
81 Bloomingdale Rd, Hicksville
NY 11801, USA
Tel. 516-933-1000, Fax: 516-933-1200
Toll Free: 1-888-560-3222
email: info@ibpublisher.com
www.ibpublisher.com

Printed in India

Prologue

Welcome to the Hussein family house, where Fatima, Hamza, A'isha and little Ali live with their parents, Sarah and Mustafa Hussein. The ten year old twins, Hamza and A'isha are playing upstairs with their new jigsaw puzzle; Fatima, who is thirteen, is busy memorising from the Quran. In his bedroom, which is opposite Mum and Dad's, we find little 3 year old Ali having his nap. Dad, a popular teacher in the local primary school is in the study, marking his class's work and Mum will be back soon from her evening shift as a nurse at the children's hospital.

But let's leave them alone for now. Later they will take you on an exciting journey towards exploring the life of Prophet Muhammad ﷺ and show you how we can live like our beloved Prophet. I am sure this family will inspire you to love the Prophet and Allah's religion more, insha'Allah.

These stories will unfold the wonderful personality of one of the most successful men in the history of the world and shed light on some of his qualities such as courage, hard work, responsibility, compassion, faith, honesty, loyalty, friendship and many more.

The Prophet's Forefathers

Haya Hassan

On a bright Saturday afternoon, Fatima, A'isha and Hamza were at their local Islamic school. Ali was at home with Mum, Dad and Granddad. Granddad was visiting for the week and the kids were very excited. Little Ali was waiting impatiently for his brother and sisters to return from Saturday school and play with him. An hour later, Fatima, A'isha and Hamza returned from the Islamic school and found Mum cooking dinner, they ran up to her and said, "Assalamu Alaykum, Mum!"

Mum hugged them and replied "Wa Alaykumus-Salam, how was your day?"

"Great," all three replied together and Mum smiled. The children learnt a lot about Islam at their Saturday school and always had a lot of fun. The boys sat down to drink a glass of milk and Fatima told her mother about the new project that she was assigned at Saturday school. It was due in a couple of days, Mum suggested she should start early. The children ate their snacks and went upstairs; the twins went to their room to play with their new jigsaw puzzles.

The First House of Worship

The Kabah is the first house of worship. Allah says in the Quran: "The first House to be built for mankind was the one at Bakkah [Makkah]. It is a blessed place; a source of guidance for the whole world." (3:96)

Who first built the Kabah?

a. Angels

b. The Prophet Ibrahim عليه السلام

c. The Prophet Ibrahim عليه السلام and the Prophet Ismail عليه السلام

Answer: c

Fatima ran up to her room and started her exciting project. An hour passed and Fatima was waiting for the black paint to dry. Suddenly Ali rushed into her room. He was looking for his smallest teddy that he had left the day before. Ali saw a black box, shining because of fresh reflecting paint next to his teddy. Filled with curiosity, Ali poked his little fingers into the box to find out what was inside it.

Fatima was washing her hands in the bathroom and when she came back to her room, she exclaimed: "Stop Ali, that's my

Hadith

Islam has been built on five pillars: shahadah, performance of prayers, pilgrimage to the Kabah, fasting during Ramadan, and paying zakah.

Bukhari and Muslim

project!"

Ali pulled his hand back quickly. "I was just looking! What is this Fatima?" he asked. "It just looks like a boring black box!"

Fatima smiled. She was always very patient with Ali and tried to explain what she was making, "It's a special model called the Kabah."

Before Fatima had finished her sentence, Granddad came into the room. The children had spent very little time with him today as they had been at school. Granddad looked at the box and guessed that it was a model of the Kabah and guessed that Fatima was trying to explain to Ali what the Kabah was. He called A'isha and Hamza into the room as well, "Hey kids, come here, and I'll tell you a story about how Allah protected his house, the Kabah. First of all though, who can tell me what the Kabah is?"

Fatima answered, "I know! We learnt today that the Kabah is the holiest place for Muslims, surrounded by a mosque called 'Masjid al Haram'. All Muslims pray towards the Kabah."

Granddad nodded and smiled, "Good Fatima, do you know who built it?"

"Yes, I know," said A'isha. "The Prophet Ibrahim عليه السلام and his son the Prophet Ismail عليه السلام."

"Well done," said Granddad, "MashAllah, you all know a lot about Islam. I'll tell you a special story from the Quran about how Allah protected the Kabah from the evil people." The kids listened attentively.

"During the time of the Prophet Muhammad's ﷺ grandfather, Abdul Muttalib, there was an Abyssinian governor of Sana, the capital of Yemen, named Abraha. He was jealous of the fact that a large number of people visited Makkah for pilgrimage. He planned to stop the people from going to the Kabah for this purpose, and ordered his people to build a huge Kannesa (building) so high that they would have to bend their heads back to be able to see its top. He thought that if the building was bigger and more beautiful than the Kabah, people would come on pilgrimage to his building rather than to the Kabah. But, to his dismay, no one really ever came. In fact a

man actually defiled Abraha's building. Out of rage and jealousy, he set out to destroy the Kabah."

"He was a very mean man!" exclaimed little Ali.

Granddad nodded and continued his story. "So he prepared a huge army of elephants, horses, camels, and a large number of soldiers to destroy the Kabah. He even asked the king of Ethiopia to join him, so the Ethiopian king sent him his strongest elephant to ride on and lead the army. Abraha himself led the army and rode on the back of this huge, strong elephant. Once they were all ready, the army marched towards Makkah.

Now, the Kabah was under the care of the Prophet's grandfather, who was also the leader of the tribe.

"A'isha, do you remember the name of the Prophet's grandfather?"

"I know! Abdul Muttalib! Isn't that it, Granddad?" she replied.

"Yes, A'isha. Well done! His name was Abdul Muttalib. He was a very kind and respectable man. He always treated his tribe with justice and was very popular among his people.

Abraha halted his army and sent his people forward to the outskirts of Makkah. His people took what they could find on their way, and this included 200 camels belonging to Abdul Muttalib. Abdul Muttalib came to Abraha and asked for his camels to be returned. Abraha was surprised to hear the chief asking only for his camels, instead of worrying that his army was heading to destroy the Kabah. Abdul Muttalib replied to Abrahra's query, "I am the lord of these camels, and likewise, the Kabah has a Lord that will defend it." Abraha returned Abdul Muttalib's camels and the chief went to his people, ordering them to retreat to the mountain side above the town.

Makkah in the Quran

Makkah is mentioned in the Quran by different names, The Quran calls it Makkah in Surah Al-Fath (48:24), safe sanctuary in Surah Al-Ankabut (29:67),city of peace in Surah Al-Baqarah (2:126), city in Surah Al- Balad (90:1-3), secure land in Surah Al- Tin (95:3) and is also mentioned as Bakkah in Surah Al-Imran (3:96).

In the morning, when the army marched closer to Makkah, an amazing thing happened: the strong elephants suddenly stopped and would not move any further! Abraha

> Have you not seen how your Lord dealt with the people of the elephant? Did He not foil their strategy and send against them flocks of birds, which pelted them with clay stones? Thus He made them like stubble cropped by cattle?
>
> *Al-Fil 105:1-5*

and his soldiers were very angry, and pulled and pushed the elephants, but they wouldn't even move a single step."

"Wow, this must be from Allah." said Hamza confidently.

"Yes, you are right, dear," said their Granddad, and he continued with his story.

"Abraha ordered the army to march forward without the elephants. Then, another amazing thing happened. All of a sudden, Allah sent a huge flock of small birds called '*Ababeel*'(Swallows). They covered the whole sky and each bird was carrying three pebbles. When they threw down the pebbles, the pebbles worked like bullets and pierced the soldiers' bodies and knocked down the whole army of powerful elephants, camels and horses. The whole army of Abraha was destroyed and the Kabah was unharmed. "The people in Makkah cheered and were happy that Allah had saved their people and had protected the Kabah."

A'isha, Hamza and Fatima cheered, but little Ali looked scared. Ali said, "Oh dear, I hope Allah will not send birds to throw stones at me because I poked the Kabah!"

Granddad hugged Ali and comforted him, "Oh no Ali, Allah loves the children who learn about Islam. You know, Allah tells us different stories in the Quran to teach us different things. With this story, we learn that no matter how strong the enemy is, we must not fear them and should have faith in Allah, as He is all-powerful, and He can protect us in ways we least expect." Ali hugged his Granddad and ran up to Fatima and hugged her too, "Please, can I help you in your project, Fatima? It looks very exciting."

Fatima replied, "Of course you can, Ali." Granddad smiled and left the children helping Fatima to complete her Kabah project.

The Early Life

Hibah Hassan and Haya Hassan

It was a rainy Friday evening. Mum was at the hospital on her evening shift, so Dad and Grandfather were at home looking after everyone. The children were being very rowdy and making a lot of noise and Dad and Grandfather were having a hard time trying to calm them down.

Suddenly, Dad had an idea. He called all the kids into the living room and asked them to sit down and listen to his plan for the weekend.

Dad said, "Everyone sit down. Let's have a quiz, and if you do well, I'll take you to the zoo tomorrow."

All of the children were very excited and A'isha hung on to her father's arm and whispered, "Please say the quiz will be about the Prophet Muhammad ﷺ, because Mum read a very nice book about him to us a few days ago."

Hamza, Ali and Fatima all agreed with A'isha. "Okay then," said Dad, "let's make teams."

So Dad put Fatima and Ali in 'Team A', and A'isha and Hamza in 'Team B'.

Granddad was to ask the first question, "Hmm…" he thought, "Okay, the first question is for everyone. What was the year called in which the Prophet was born?"

The children all shouted together,

"The year of the elephant!"

Granddad smiled and applauded them for remembering this from the day before.

Granddad put the next question to Fatima and Ali. "Okay! Your question is: What was the name of the Prophet Muhammad's ﷺ father?"

The Month of Rabi ul Awwal

Prophet Muhammad was born in Makkah in the month of Rabi ul Awwal. It was the same year when the Abraha came to destroy Kaaba with his huge army. What was the year called:

a. The Year of Blessing
b. The Year of Elephant
c. The Year of War

Answer: b

Hadith

God has more compassion for His servants than a woman does for her child.

Muslim

Hamza's hand shot up and he said impatiently, "I know! I know! His name was Abdullah!"

Granddad nodded, "Well done, Hamza! Okay, now, team B… What was the name of the Prophet's mother?"

Ali shouted out loudly, "Her name was Amina! I have a friend at school and her name is Amina. She told me that she was named after the Prophet's mother."

Granddad nodded. "Good job, Ali! Alright, so both teams have one point each."

Now it was Dad's turn. First he told the children a fact by asking, "Did you know that the Prophet Muhammad ﷺ, father died before he was born?" Fatima nodded to show that she knew this.

Then he asked the first team, "Team A, can you tell me how old the Prophet was when his mother passed away?"

Fatima answered correctly, "He was 6 years old," she said.

Good, Fatima. Now, team B, after his mother's death, who took care of the Prophet?"

A'isha asked, "Umm, was it his grandfather, Abdul Muttalib?"

Dad nodded, "Yes, well done, A'isha! Now both teams have two points each!"

It was Granddad's turn again, "Team A, at what age did the Prophet Muhammad's ﷺ Uncle take custody of him?"

Ali looked at Fatima. "Fatima," he whispered, "I don't know the answer. Can you tell me?" Fatima nodded. "Nine," she whispered back. Ali shouted, "Nine years! The Prophet was nine when his uncle started to take care of him."

"That's right Ali," Granddad chuckled and then asked,

"What was the name of the Prophet's uncle who took care of him after the death of his grandfather? During the early years of Islam, when all the Makkans stood against our dear Prophet, his uncle protected him and took care of him."

Team B was quick to reply, "His name was Abu Talib."

The quiz continued until Mum came back. When she returned from the hospital, she found all of the children crowded around Dad and their Granddad, listening eagerly. Granddad said that both the teams had done very well and Dad announced that tomorrow the whole family would go to the zoo.

It was a very informative evening for the children, as they had also learnt about the early life of the Prophet Muhammad ﷺ in the desert. They learnt that it was the tradition of the Arabian tribes to send their sons to be weaned in the desert, as people believed that the desert air would help them to grow strong and healthy. They found out that a lady called Halima chose to take care for the Prophet Muhammad ﷺ.
She was not a rich lady, and only owned one goat and a she-camel. The camel was not giving enough milk for the family as there was a drought, but the day Halima took the Prophet Muhammad ﷺ away with her, the camel suddenly started to give a lot of milk and Halima was able to feed the Prophet and her own son as well. The years that the Prophet Muhammad ﷺ spent with Halima were filled with blessings and happiness for her and her family.

Halimah as Sadiyyah

Halimah Sadiyyah was an Arab bedouin woman. She was a wet-nurse who took care of Prophet Muhammad ﷺ in the early years of his life. Halimah decided to take care of the Prophet when other wet nurses refused to take care of him because he was an orphan. After Halima decided to take care of the Prophet, she witnessed many blessings of Allah in her life. She loved the Prophet dearly and so did the Prophet. The Prophet Muhammad ﷺ also respected her a lot.

'Did He not find you orphaned and shelter you? Did He not find you wandering, and give you guidance? Did He not find you in want, and make you free from want? Therefore do not treat the orphan with harshness, and do not chide the one who asks for help; but proclaim the blessings of your Lord'

Al-Duha 93:6-11

Ali was delighted to hear about the camel and he excitedly asked Fatima if he would see a camel at the zoo tomorrow. Fatima laughed, "Maybe you will, Ali! But I want to see a tiger, they are such beautiful animals!" Hamza agreed, "I want to see an elephant too!"

The children all went to bed thinking of what they had learnt about the Prophet and the animals they would see at the zoo.

A Mercy to Animals

Zineb Sarah Messaoui

"Wake up, Fatima! Remember, we're going to visit the zoo today!" Hamza said.

At this, Fatima's eyes fluttered open. Instead of groaning as usual, she happily jumped out of bed remembering the zoo. A'isha did not like animals but Hamza, on the other hand, enjoyed teasing them. Then there was little Ali, who like Fatima, was fascinated by all animals.

Soon, everyone jumped into the car and arrived at the zoo. The children started fighting over which animal to visit first, so the parents chose the elephant. Ali was amazed by the size and strength of the creature, and Hamza and Fatima expressed how they'd love to ride one. "Is it true that the elephant's skin is very tough?" asked A'isha. Dad was about to answer when Hamza cut in. "Want to see? I'll show you." And with that, he threw a pebble at the elephant. Mum stopped him at once and made him apologise for such cruelty. Hamza hung his head and grumbled. "It's just an animal."

Abu Hurairah

Abu Hurairah is a famous companion and has narrated the most of the hadiths He was given the name "Abu Hurayrah" meaning, "Father of kittens", because in his childhood he had a cat and loved playing with cats. Abu Hurairah loved knowledge just as he loved the Prophet. He devoted his life memorising the sayings and instructions of the Prophet Muhhamad ﷺ.

Hadith

Allah will not be merciful to those who are not merciful to others.

Bukhari and Muslim

Dad shook his head in despair and said: "Let's go sit down, shall we?"

"Let me share a story that the Prophet Muhammad ﷺ told his companions, which might make you think a bit about what you did," said his father, frowning at his elder son. "OK," said Hamza, feeling sorry.

"A long time ago there was a woman who owned a cat. She was cruel and kept the cat locked up with no food or water." "Poor cat!" Fatima interrupted. Dad nodded, "She didn't even let the poor animal eat the insects off the floor! Unfortunately, the cat died... " Ali was now close to tears, "How could she treat her pet so badly," he exclaimed in disgusted.

"Did you know, our blessed Prophet Muhammadﷺ

revealed that the wicked woman would go to a very horrible place? Can you guess where?" asked Dad. "Jail?" suggested Hamza. "No," answered his father solemnly. "Hellfire..."

Mum, who had been listening, decided to explain a little more. "You see, children, Prophet Muhammad ﷺ loved and protected all animals." She wanted her children to understand the importance of not harming animals and continued,

"There was once a lady who had committed a grave sin. One day, she passed by a well and saw a dog panting with thirst. She felt sorry and decided to help. So she took off her shoe, tied it to her head scarf and lowered it into the well. She collected enough water to satisfy its thirst."

"That was very kind of her," said A'isha.

"Allah liked her actions so much that He forgave her great sin!" exclaimed Mum.

The little group had fallen silent. "Dad, I am so ashamed of myself, I want to make Allah happy with me, not displeased! I didn't mean to be cruel, I promise I won't do it again!" Hamza said.

"It's not me you have to apologise to, but Allah," smiled Dad.

The rest of the day was greatly enjoyed and passed rapidly. Hamza was careful not to harm any of Allah's amazing creatures, even accidentally!

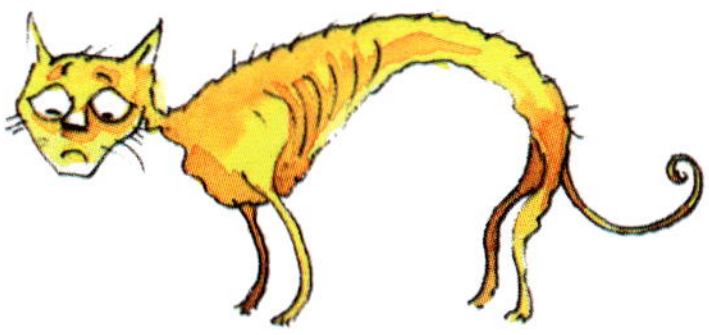

A Wise Youth

Ameena Golding

Hamza had finally convinced his parents to buy him a game console, but now he spent all his spare time playing his new game, "Super-Car Racer 2000". He was trying for the gold trophy, but so far he had been unsuccessful.

"Hamza!" called Mum, "Dinner is ready."

"Wait a second, Mum, I'm trying to get my highest score," he replied, starting another race.

"Hamza, please come down. Your dinner is getting cold," Mum called him, up the stairs. "But Mum," Hamza whined, "I was so close, I think I can do it this time." "Hamza, come down now!" Mum's tone had turned serious. "Yes Mum," grumbled Hamza, making his way down the stairs. Still thinking about the games, Hamza completely forgot to start eating the food with the name of Allah. "Hamza," said Mum sternly, "have you forgotten to say something?" Suddenly, Hamza remembered. "Oh, I forgot to say Bismillah (In the name of Allah)!" "Don't worry," replied Mum, "Allah will forgive you because you forgot. But try not to forget it again. You know the Prophet Muhammad ﷺ would not start eating or drinking before he said 'Bismillah'. He would also end his meal by thanking Allah."

Hamza started to feel guilty. "I'm sorry. I will really try from now on." "It's okay," replied Mum. "Have you done your homework?" Hamza had been

Trading Goods

Khadijah, a rich Makkan merchant, employed the Prophet Muhammad ﷺ to sell her goods. She sent her servant Maysarah with the prophet as an escort. The Prophet worked honestly and returned to Makkah with a good profit. Which country did the Prophet and Maysarah go to?

a. Yemen
b. Syria
c. Egypt

Answer: b

Hadith

The most superior among you are those who learn the Quran and teach it to others.

Bukhari

so immersed in his game that he had completely forgotten about it. “Oops, I forgot...” he mumbled. “Hamza, you’re spending too much time on that games console,” said Mum sternly. “I’m starting to regret buying it! If you continue to neglect your homework, then your Dad and I will have no choice but to put it away.” Hamza panicked at the thought of losing his precious game,

“I’m really sorry Mum, it won’t happen again, I promise.”

In the classroom, Hamza stared blankly at the blackboard, not really paying attention to what his science teacher was saying. His thoughts soon drifted to Super-Car Racer 2000, “if I pretend I’m going to study, Mum will let me go up to my room after school, and then I can play the game! No, I can’t do that... that’s lying to Mum... but I really want to get that gold trophy... what Mum doesn’t know won’t hurt her, right?” Hamza’s thoughts were suddenly interrupted by the shrill voice of the teacher, “Hamza!” “Um, y-yes Mrs.Richards?” replied Hamza nervously. “Are you paying attention?” she snapped. “Y-yes miss,” lied Hamza, “Well then, can you please tell us what we have been discussing?”

“Um... wasn’t it something about, um, the w-water cycle? Hamza mumbled, glancing at his friend Zuhair’s notes.

“Hm, good,” Mrs. Richards replied, slightly surprised. Hamza, on the other hand, felt guilty about cheating. “I really should have paid attention in class, like Zuhair,” Hamza thought to himself, staring at his desk in shame and fiddling around with a half-chewed pencil.

Still, once home, he decided to put his plan into action. He rushed upstairs into his room and turned on the games console. Quite a long while later, Hamza yawned and glanced at his watch.

It was 6:00pm. “Wow, have I really been sitting up here playing this game for a whole two hours?

I should stop... but how can I? I haven’t even gotten the gold trophy yet!” Suddenly he heard footsteps outside his room and the door burst open. Mum stood there, looking disappointed. “Hamza, please sit here with me,” she beckoned.

“Hamza, I know you’ve been spending a lot of time

on this game lately, and it's showing in your grades. I just got a phone call from your English teacher. She tells me that you didn't hand in your assignment"

"Mum, I'm really sorry, it's just that I really wanted to get the gold trophy..." Hamza trailed off. "I know you do, but tell me what is going to have a bigger and better impact on your life? Getting knowledge and good grades, or getting a gold trophy that isn't even real?" Mum looked at Hamza and could tell that he was sorry. "Now, let me tell you about the Prophet Muhammad ﷺ when he was a young boy. Do you know what he would do? Hamza nodded,

"He would go with his uncle to the market and learn about trading, and how to behave with adults." Mum continued,

"You know, Hamza, the Prophet was a shepherd like many other great Prophets, such as Jesus and Moses. Allah chose this work for a reason. Can you think why?"

Hamza started thinking, "Since Allah loved His Prophet, He chose an easy job for him, as shepherd don't do much work."

"Well it seems as if a shepherd's job is easy but it's not. It's a very tough job. Every day they have to take a herd of sheep to the mountains and make sure they are safe from wild animals. They must be fed and kept together. Sheep tend to stray away from the flock. You know Allah prepares his prophets for the tough tasks ahead."

"Hmm, I can see what you mean. Prophets protect their people from going astray," remarked Hamza.

"Correct, Hamza, you are very clever!"

Hamza was feeling ashamed of his behaviour, but at the same time enjoying Mum's conversation.

"Did the Prophet Muhammad ﷺ work all his life as a shepherd? asked Hamza.

"He worked as a shepherd for a few years, then he worked as a merchant. He used to take goods

Ali ibn Abi Talib

Ali, the fourth caliph was the son of Abi Talib and was a cousin of the Prophet. Ali was the first youth to enter Islam. He was respected for his courage, knowledge, and unflinching devotion to Islam. Ali lived a very simple life. He was also the son-in-law of the Prophet, husband of his beloved daughter, Fatima. One of Ali's important task was to write letters to people on behalf of the Prophet.

I swear by the passage of time, that man is surely in a state of loss, except for those who believe and do good deeds and exhort one another to hold fast to the Truth, and who exhort one another to steadfastness.

Al-'Asr 103:1-3

from one city to another and sell them. With his hard and honest work, the Prophet Muhammad ﷺ earned the title of "Al-Ameen". Among the Makkans, a rich lady, Khadija, approached the Prophet to work for her."

Hamza was listening attentively as Mum continued,

"His hard work and honesty impressed Khadija so much that she later married him. So you see, Hamza? The Prophet Muhammad ﷺ spent his time as a youth wisely, so that he was prepared for his years as an adult." Mum looked at Hamza, who had been listening intently to everything Mum had been saying.

"Yeah, you're right, Mum. What am I doing, spending so much time on this game? Sorry... I just got distracted," mumbled Hamza.

"It's okay Hamza, we all make mistakes in life, but we learn from them too. Remember Allah says in the Quran that anyone who works hard will be rewarded," said Mum, hugging Hamza. "Thanks Mum.

I should do my homework now," laughed Hamza.

A few days have passed since Hamza's conversation with Mum. Now, he only plays for a few hours on the weekends. He finishes his homework on time and pays attention in class. One day Hamza walked into his science class, nervously waited as Mrs. Richards handed out their science grades. Hamza was thrilled - he had actually gotten an A! "Wow, it turns out that hard work really does pay off!" he thought. Just as everyone was about to leave class, Mrs. Richards announced that she would be giving out prizes to students who had improved the most in their studies. This week's prize winner was Hamza! Hamza's eyes widened as Mrs Richards pulled out a giant bag of jelly-beans from her handbag. Hamza eagerly rushed up to claim his prize. "Thank you, Miss," he said, hugging the bag of jelly-beans, "It turns out that a bit of hard work isn't so bad after all!"

A Peacemaker

Zineb Sarah Messaoui

"I want it!" screamed Ali. "No! It's mine!" yelled back Hamza. "I'm the oldest, I should have it," complained Fatima. A'isha burst into tears, "Why can't we all have it!" she sobbed.

Dad walked into the room: "Calm down everyone," he said firmly. Then he asked kindly, "What's the matter? And please talk one at a time," he said, noticing each child was about to start shouting again.

Hamza started, "Uncle Mahmood gave us a skipping rope and, you know Dad, it's new in the market. It can be a hula-hoop and become longer and shorter. We all want to play with it!"

"We can't all play at the same time..." exclaimed Ali. Dad sighed. He put Ali on one knee, A'isha on the other and told the other two to sit down.

"Hmmm.... I understand, I can see it's a very special rope and you all want to play with it now. But don't you think it would be much better if we try to find a way that can please everyone and Allah? This fighting and snatching might break your new rope and then you'll be left with nothing to play with," explained Dad.

The kids nodded in agreement, "But how can we all play at one time?" asked A'isha

"Okay, if we have an argument, what do you think is the best way to find a solution?"

He looked at kids and asked.

Hamza said proudly, "I remember our Quran teacher taught us to look in the Quran first".

The Tribe of the Prophet

When the Prophet Muhammad ﷺ was born, Arabs were divided into tribes and further into clans. People were respected according to the strength of the tribe. Which tribe Prophet Muhammad's family belonged to:

a. Banu Hashim
b. Banu Abd Shams
c. Banu Thaqif

Answer: a

Hadith

None of you believes until he wishes for his brother what he wishes for himself

Bukhari

Ali said, "Does the Quran tell us how to play with toys too?"

Dad smiled and replied, "Ali, the Quran tells you how to lead your life, just as in school you have books, but, at the same time, you need a teacher to explain to you what is in the book and how you can benefit from it. In the same way, the Quran is the textbook and the Prophet is the teacher. Let's see what the Prophet did when he faced a situation a little like yours."

The kids were getting curious and listened attentively. Dad started... "You know, our blessed Prophet Muhammad ﷺ was a peacemaker. Whenever there was a conflict, he would try to find a clever solution to the problem that would bring people together. Have you heard the story of the placement of the black stone?" he asked the children. They shook their heads and Ali pleaded, "Tell us Dad!"

"Once, the Kabah was damaged by a fire, and all the tribes of Makkah helped to rebuild it. But, when it was time to put the black stone back in place, each of the four leaders of the Makkan tribes wanted to have this honour. So, an argument broke out."

"But Dad," interrupted A'isha, "What's so special about the black stone?"

Dad answered, "It's a stone sent from heaven to the Prophet Adam عليه السلام. Later on, the Prophet Ibrahim عليه السلام set it to mark the spot from where to start tawaf. It was considered sacred by the Makkans." Dad went on, "As they could not come to an agreement, they decided that the first person to enter the Kabah would choose who should put the black stone back in place. You know who entered first? The Prophet Muhammad ﷺ! So the Makkans exclaimed joyfully, 'Al- Ameen! (the trustworthy)', as it was the nickname given to him due to his honesty. The Prophet Muhammad ﷺ gave them a clever solution. He placed the stone on a white sheet then instructed each of the four clans' leaders to hold one corner and carry the stone to its place. Then Prophet Muhammad ﷺ himself lifted the stone from the sheet and put in position."

"Wow! great idea!" admired Fatima.

"Yes," agreed the others.

"But," whispered Ali "We still don't know who should use the skipping rope first."

"Sometimes," Dad said, "To make peace you have to make a few sacrifices." Seeing the confused faces of the children, he decided to tell them another story. "Have you heard of the treaty of Hudaibiya?" he questioned. "I think—wasn't it a peace treaty between the disbelievers in Makkah and the Muslims, at the time of the Prophet?" asked Fatima.

"You got it," smiled Dad, "At the time when the Prophet lived in Madinah, he decided to make a trip to his hometown, Makkah, to perform Hajj (pilgrimage) with a group of followers. The people of the Quraysh, not far from the holy city, at a place called Hudaibiya, stopped the caravan. The Muslims camped there and sent a go-between, Usman, to reach an agreement.

But no agreement could be reached. Later, a few people from Makkah came to the Prophet with some conditions to resolve the situation. The Messenger of Allah then signed a treaty with the Quraysh, according to which they would return to Madinah that year without performing the pilgrimage but would return the next year to do it. In return, the Quraysh promised to keep peace for ten years. Another condition was that if any Makkan, having converted to Islam came to Madinah for protection, the Muslims would return him to the Makkans but the Makkans would not return anyone coming back to them."

"How unfair!" exclaimed Fatima.

"Indeed it was unfair. But the Prophet of Allah accepted the condition as he preferred peace to war... You see, to sign that truce was quite a difficult decision as many of the Prophet's companions were upset over the truce. But, at the same point, Allah revealed to the Prophet that it was the right decision and that soon the Muslims

The Title of Al-Farooq

Umar ibn al-Khattab was the second Caliph of Islam and a close Companion of the Prophet. He was foremost in matters of knowledge and learning. The Prophet conferred on him the title of Al-Farooq, meaning "The separator between truth and falsehood" as he was very famous for his justice. Once the Prophet said, "Allah has placed truth upon Umar's tongue and heart."

God has in all truth shown His Messenger a true vision in which He said, 'God willing, you will most certainly enter the Sacred Mosque in safety and without fear, shaven-headed or with hair cut short'—God knew what you did not; and has given you a victory beforehand.

Al- Fath 48:27

would be victorious." Dad added.

"You know, children, just one year later, due to this peace treaty, the Muslims got a chance to concentrate on spreading the peaceful teachings of Islam around Arabia and the number of Muslims grew from 1000 to 10,000. The following year, Makkah was conquered without any bloodshed. Do you know what the Prophet did when he entered Makkah, where he and his companions had been persecuted and driven out? He declared peace and forgave all." finished Dad, looking at his children.

"Now who will suggest the solution to your problem?" asked Dad.

"Maybe Fatima and I can hold the rope and make A'isha and Ali jump," suggested Hamza with his eyes lowered.

"Yes! Then we can switch." said Fatima happily. Dad knew that it was difficult for them to say this. "Later we can all try the hula hoop and see who can keep it longest!" declared A'isha, delighted.

"I am so pleased with my little peacemakers." Dad said with a wink.

A Kind Master

Haya Hassan

It was the summer holidays and the Hussein family had decided to go on a vacation to Pakistan to visit their extended family. The children were very excited to see their Aunty Fareeda and Uncle Usman and their dear cousins at the airport. Their Aunty had two daughters and one son; Sumaiya, Khadija and Zain. Fatima, the twins and Ali always had a lot of fun in Pakistan with their cousins.

Aunty Fareeda had prepared a delicious lunch at home that ended with their favorite sweets, gulab jammon and ras malai.

"Oh, I love these!" said Fatima, helping herself to a second serving.

After lunch, Mum gave everyone their presents that they had brought from England; Mum had also got a special present, a handbag, for Amal, who helped aunty with her housework.

During their stay, the Husseins noticed the disrespectful behavior of their cousin towards Amal. They often shouted at her and treated her unkindly.

"Hey, where did you put my scarf now?" shouted Sumaiya one day.

"It's in your cupboard," replied Amal patiently.

"No, it's not there. You come here and give it to me!" shouted Sumaiya.

Amal left her work and got the scarf out from Sumaiya's cupboard. Rather than being ashamed of her shouting, she snatched it from Amal and said, "I didn't see it. You always put my stuff in different places."

The First Muadhhin

When Bilal Ibn Rabah was from the Habasha clan of black race. He was the slave of Ummayah Ibn Khalif and he tortured Bilal immensely to turn him away from Islam. Which companion bought him and made him a free man?

a. Abu Bakr
b. Jafar bin Abi Talib
c. Amr bin Auf

Answer: a

Hadith

No one eats better food than that which he eats out of the work of his own hand.

Bukhari

Amal went downstairs without saying anything.

The next day Khadija needed a glass, and she screamed "Give me a glass now!"

"Sorry, Khadija, I'm washing the dishes, my hands are wet. Please take it yourself," said Amal.

"No! You give it to me, I need it for my Aunty," said Khadija angrily.

Amal left the dishes and went to the cupboard and got out a glass and gave it to Khadija, She snatched it from Amal then went out of the kitchen without saying thank you.

Amal had been getting very upset with this rude behaviour and was thinking of looking for some other work. She loved the children, but they were ill-mannered with her. Despite her kind treatment of the children, she was not respected.

She was very kind and patient with the children but still they never respected her Aunty Fareeda often reprimanded the children for being rude to Amal, but they ignored this.

For the Hussein children, this was a new experience, as they were used to doing all their work themselves. If they needed help, they always said the magic word 'Please' and never forgot to say "Thank you". One day Zain couldn't find one of his trainers and he was rude and behaved badly towards Amal once more. Amal had had enough. Making a split second decision, she decided to leave the job. She went up to Aunty Fareeda and said, "I am sorry, I do not wish to work where I am not respected."

Aunty Fareeda apologized, "I am very sorry for my children's behaviour. You are a very good person and we all like your manners and appreciate your work. Please give them a another chance."

Unfortunately, Amal did not agree, so Aunty Fareeda made her a proposition, "Why don't you take two days off and meanwhile, I will make sure that the children start behaving properly. On your return you can decide if you want to stay."

Amal agreed to this arrangement.

In the evening, Fatima suggested having a

midnight feast and the children loved the idea. Soon they were called for dinner to join the elders at the dining table. While eating, they excitedly made plans for their midnight feast. They were so busy with their plans that no one noticed that Amal wasn't there.

After dinner, they decided to play for a while and since Ali and Zain were very young and couldn't stay up till midnight, they decided to have their feast at 10pm. "It's a 10'o clock feast!" giggled Ali happily. Time flew by and at quarter to ten, the children were jumping up and down with excitement. They crept downstairs and got some cheesecake, crisps, biscuits and sweets. They were chatting and eating and having a great time.

They ended up having an energetic pillow fight when suddenly a pillow flew straight at Khadija's glass, and apple juice spilt everywhere. Khadija ran downstairs to look for Amal, but Amal was nowhere to be found. "Hamza, have you seen Amal?" she inquired.

"Maybe she has left, you have all been so rude to her," suggested Hamza meekly.

"No, we haven't been rude," exclaimed Khadija angrily.

"I think he's right. You and your brother and sister have been very unkind to Amal," added Fatima.

Khadija felt a bit ashamed of her behavior but didn't accept her mistake. So Fatima and Hamza went back upstairs.

Khadija, while cleaning up the mess, started thinking about Amal and what Hamza and Fatima had said, but her thoughts were interrupted by Fatima calling the children to hear a story. Zain and Ali were the first to climb onto the bed and the rest followed.

All the children loved stories a lot and forgot that they were sleepy.

"Who knows the story of the

Bilal Ibn Rabah

Bilal Ibn Rabah is also known as Bilal al Habashi. He was one of the most trusted and loyal companion of the Prophet. He was born in Makkah. The Prophet Muhammad chose him as the first Muaddhin (call of a prayer). Born as a slave, he later became one of the most respected companion, remembered up till today for his piety and love of Islam. He became a symbol of racial equality in Islam.

> The true servants of the Gracious One are those who walk upon the earth with humility and when they are addressed by the ignorant ones, their response is, 'Peace';
>
> *Al- Furqan 25:63*

Prophet Muhammad ﷺ and Zayd ibn Haritha, his slave?" Fatima asked, no one seemed to know.

Fatima started, "In the olden times, the people use to buy slaves to work for them. One day, Khadija, a rich businesswoman, bought a slave named 'Zayd' from the market of Makkah. He was a kind boy and worked for Khadija honestly. When Khadija got married to the Prophet Muhammad ﷺ, she gave the boy to him. The Prophet Muhammad ﷺ was very kind to Zayd and took great care of him. Zayd loved the Prophet Muhammad ﷺ in return and was very happy in his company.

When Zayd's father came to know about Zayd's whereabouts, he rushed to the Prophet's house and said, "I will give all the money you want for the release of my son."

The Prophet greeted him kindly and replied, "Let Zayd decide, if he chooses to go with you, take him without any money, but if he chooses to stay with me, why should he not?"

Zayd was called, and he chose to stay with the blessed Prophet, who treated him as if he was his own son. Zayd's father was astounded to hear that his son didn't want to live with him, "You don't want to come back to your mother or your family?"

Zayd replied quite firmly, "No, I want to live with the Prophet Muhammad ﷺ."

The Prophet Muhammad ﷺ took Zayd by his hand to the Kabah and declared Zayd to be his adopted son. Zayd's father returned home satisfied , seeing Zayd as a free person and happy with the Prophet Muhammad ﷺ. He realized how kind the Prophet Muhammad ﷺ was.

From then on, Zayd lived with the Prophet Muhammadﷺ in his house like a family mcmber."

Fatima looked at her cousins and asked, "You know Zayd ibn Haritha was the first slave to accept Islam." She added sleepily, "We better go to sleep now", Ali and Zain were already half asleep in a corner of the bed.

The next morning around breakfast, they inquired about Amal. Aunty Fareeda replied sternly, "She left because as you were very unkind to her."

"We want her back, please call her," pleaded the children.

"We'll talk about it later, let's eat." replied Aunty Fareeda.

After eating, the kids had to clean and wash the dishes. While working, they realized that they had never helped Amal, but had rather created more work for her. And so, Aunty Fareeda assigned duties to the children around the house.

"Since Amal has left, Sumayya you can make all the beds, Khadija will clear up all the clothes and Zain will tidy up the toys upstairs."

The Hussein children offered to help but Aunty Fareeda politely refused. All the cleaning made the children tired and more ashamed of their behavior.

Aunty Fareeda made some fresh mango lassi (mango curd shake) and called the children into the living room after they had finished all the chores.

The lassi was very refreshing after all the work. While drinking it, Aunty Fareeda started telling them about the companion of the Prophet.

Set Free Slaves

Abu Bakr, the first Caliph was a rich man and was famous for his good character and generous nature. After converting to Islam, he used his money for defending and helping fellow Muslims. He purchased and set free many slaves. The first muezzin of Islam, Bilal Habashi, was purchased and set free by Abu Bakr. When the Prophet received the first revelation from Allah and when he was taken to the Heavens (*Al-Mi'raj*), Abu Bakr believed the Prophet and stood by him. Abu Bakr always believed the Prophet and also stood by him whether it was the first revelation which Prophet received from Allah or when he was taken to the Heavens (*Al-Miraj*) Thus, he earned the title of 'al-Siddiq', which means a very strong and honest friend. The Prophet once said, "No one has been a better companion to me than Abu Bakr."

"You know, once a man came to the Prophet and asked, "O Messenger of Allah, to what extent should we forgive the mistakes of our slaves or servants?" The Prophet remained silent. The man repeated the enquiry, and the Prophet again remained silent. When he asked for the third time, the Prophet replied, "Seventy times each day.""

"Wow! Seventy times and we get impatient if Amal makes one small mistake!" Summaiya was feeling guilty.

The children were listening attentively, and Aunty Fareeda continued, "On another occasion, the Prophet said, "whoever has a slave should feed him and clothe him as does for himself. And he should not make work from a slave that is beyond his powers, And if he does tell him to do a difficult job, he should join in to help the slave."

"But Mum, Amal is not a slave, she's just a maid," Khadija interrupted.

"Hmm, a maid. Can you tell me, Khadija, who is a maid? Isn't she doing a job like your Dad?" asked Mum.

"Sort of," Khadija replied. She was getting Mum's point.

"It's exactly the same, just as your Dad has a job to earn his living, Amal is doing a job to earn her living and it's your duty to be kind and polite to her, as taught by our dear Prophet." explained Aunty Fareeda. "You see, nowadays slavery has been abolished, Alhamdulillah. But all the teachings of the Prophet apply to all the employees doing any work. Maids are doing a job for you. They are helping you in household chores."

"Now tell me, do you have anything more to say?" asked their Mum.

The children nodded and replied, "We are really very sorry. Please give us a last chance. Call Amal and we will apologize to her."

Aunty Fareeda agreed to call Amal back to see if she would like to work with them again. The next day, Amal came back and all the three children simultaneously said, "Please, Amal, forgive us, we are very sorry for being rude to you." Khadija added, "We promise not to annoy you, or be rude to you again, and also help you in your work."

Amal smiled and replied, "I am glad you have realized this and, like you, I will also follow the Prophet Muhammad's ﷺ example and forgive you."

They hugged Amal and the Hussein children stood smiling along with their cousins.

An Honest Merchant

Sarah Ali

It was the summer holidays and the Hussein family was visiting their uncle in Toronto, Canada. Summer was a wonderful time to visit with, flowers and glorious maple trees everywhere.

"Thank you for inviting us, dear brother," Mum smiled at Uncle Ridwan. "It's my pleasure!" With that, Uncle Ridhwan picked Ali up and twirled him around in the air.

They were interrupted by a loud voice rumbling across the street.

"-LEMONADE! LEMONADE!! Only 50 cents a glass!! LEMONADE!"

"Lemonade sounds good, shall we get a glass each?" Uncle said, handing them the money. The kids rushed outside to a large lemonade stand. Two girls and a boy were selling the lemonade.

"Assalamualykum, I'm Asma," introduced the older girl. "Walykumussalam, I'm Fatima and these are the twins," Fatima replied.

" A'isha and Hamza!" The twins said together, laughing.

"I'm Ali!" Ali exclaimed.

"Welcome! I'm Nur," the younger girl smiled. "Would you like to buy lemonade?"

"Six glasses, please!" the twins said simultaneously.

Nur laughed, "Cool!" The little boy, Rashid approached the group shyly and took the money.

The children left happily with lemonade that was extra delicious in the warm afternoon.

Later that day, the children approached Mum, "Mum, can we please go to Marine land? It's an amazing water park where you can see killer whales and sea lions. There is even a Dolphin Shows where the dolphins perform!" A'isha added excitedly.

"There are many amusement park rides to

On the Way to Madinah

Who encountered the Prophet Muhammad ﷺ and Abu Bakr during their migration to Madinah and wanted to capture them for the reward?

a. Suraqah bin Ju'shum
b. Khalid bin Waleed
c. Abu Jahl

Answer: a

Hadith

Give
the worker
his wages before his
sweat dries.

Ibn Majah

go on too! We can save enough money for our tickets by selling things," Hamza continued enthusiastically.

"I saw some old toys in the attic that Uncle Ridhwan intended to throw out. He has allowed us to use them." Fatima explained.

"Can we please go as soon as we've saved enough money?" Ali asked.

Mum smiled, "Hmm, that's an excellent idea, however, this will be have to be your project, without any help from adults."

The kids agreed and went straight to work. After a laborious week, it was time for the stall to be opened. Everyone tried their hardest to make the toys look better than they really were by wrapping the toys in colourful boxes with false labels.

The first customer was Mrs Alam, their neighbour.

She decided to buy a Barbie doll for $20, in a colourful box labeled "Talking doll", though in reality, the speaker was broken. Mrs. Alam also bought a package labeled 'badminton set with two rackets and 3 shuttlecocks' (also untrue) for $23.The Hussein kids made $43 from their first customer!

Next came Mr Ahsan with his children, who purchased the '3 in 1 Pirate Bears Set', for $35. Afrah bought a football, which was almost brand-new, for $35 too.

It was only the first day and the children had made $113 altogether!

The next day, the children were certain of making more profits. However, Mrs. Alam returned, and looking extremely dissatisfied said, "I believe I have been deceived. I paid $43 for these toys," she held up her purchases, the doll was in a terrible state. She then held up her badminton bag and took out everything: there was a broken badminton racket, a tennis racket, and three broken shuttlecocks.

Reluctantly, Hamza handed Mrs. Alam her $43 back.

Soon after, Mr. Ahsan arrived with the same outraged expression as Mrs. Alam. He held up three mutated teddy bears. One had a rag over his eye because he was one-eyed, one had a doorknob replacing its hand, messily attached with duct tape, and the last had a toothbrush as a leg. Again, they returned the money.

Fatima looked at her siblings, worriedly. They felt so ashamed! How could they not have realized that they were lying and cheating with their customers? They thought it was only a bit of exaggerated advertising.

"Assalamualykum." The sudden voice startled them all. They turned around to find Asma and Nur. The Hussein's felt more ashamed than ever. Nur handed them each a delicious glass of lemonade.

"In order to be good Muslims, we must be honest and just to everyone. You know our Prophet was always truthful and kind to all, he was called, *Al-Amin* (The Truthful) and *As-Sadiq* (The Trustworthy). A rich widow, Sayyidah Khadija had a big trading

Khadijah Bint Khuwaylid

Khadijah was the first wife of the Prophet Muhammad ﷺ. She was noble in character, because of which people respected her a lot. They called her Tahira, the Pure. She was the first person to accept Islam. Khadijah stood by the Prophet like a solid rock. She not only gave her wealth for the cause of Islam, but also became personally involved in the spreading of the message of Allah. The Prophet, while speaking of Khadijah said: "The best of women in it (Paradise) is Maryam bint Imran and the best of women in it (world) is Khadijah bint Khuwaylid."

> Give full measure and weight, according to justice—We never charge a soul with more than it can bear—when you speak, observe justice, even though it concerns a close relative;
>
> *Al-An'am 6:152*

business; she needed someone to take her goods to other countries and sell them. Sayyidah Khadijah heard of Muhammad's honesty and hired him to work for her. Muhammad, along with her slave lady, Maysarah took the goods with a caravan. Muhammad was very honest during his trading expedition, he kept prices fair, informed people of the defects of the items before selling, and kept good care of the goods." Asma said.

Nur continued, "Maysarah informed the honesty of Muhammad to Khadija, who was so impressed that she proposed Muhammad to marry her! He accepted and together they lived a happy life. We should follow our Prophet's example and be fair in advertising our products."

"Woe to those who give short measure, who demand of other people full measure for themselves, but when they give by measurement or weight to others, they give them less. Do such people not realize that they will be raised up, on a fateful day." (83:1-4)

These verses refer to the people that buy goods and then sell them for much higher prices. We all will be questioned for our deeds without exception."

"What can we do now?" Ali asked, puzzled.

Nur and Asma smiled. "You can start by removing all those boxes, so people can actually see what they are buying. You can also separate toys into groups of quality, like most-used to least-used." Nur suggested.

The Husseins tried to remember all their friends' advice and thanked them.

Ashamed, Fatima, with her siblings approached Mum once again.

"Mum, we were unfair to our customers, but we didn't know! Our neighbours pointed it out to us!" Hamza said sadly. A'isha and Fatima nodded.

Mum reassured them, " My dear children! Allah is Most Merciful. Allah will surely forgive you if you repent sincerely; it was a mistake made in ignorance. Allah tells us in Quran, 'But God would not punish them while you [Prophet] were in their midst, nor would He punish them so long as they sought forgiveness.'" (8: 33)

Mum continued: "To repent, first you must realize what you have done wrong. Then, you must ask for Allah's Forgiveness sincerely. The last step is that you must promise with sincerity that you will not repeat your mistake, with that Insha'Allah, Allah will forgive you."

The kids had learned a lot in their holidays and from that day on, they promised to be honest just like the Prophet. Soon they raised more money than required, and decided to donate the surplus to charity.

The family finally went to Marineland and had a great time. Fatima, A'isha, Hamza and Ali gained more than the treat: knowledge about their beautiful religion, Islam, in a fun and interesting way!

Prayers of the Prophet Muhammad ﷺ

O Allah, I seek from You the blessing of entering the home and the blessing of leaving the home. With the name of Allah we enter and with the name of Allah we leave, and upon Allah our Lord do we trust.

O Allah, I seek refuge with Your pleasure from Your anger. I seek refuge in Your forgiveness from Your punishment. I seek refuge in You from You. I cannot count Your praises, You are as You have praised Yourself.

O Allah, guide me with those whom You have guided, and strengthen me with those whom You have given strength. Take me to Your care with those whom You have taken to Your care. Bless me in what You have given me.

I seek refuge in Allah from the accursed Satan and from the evil of this dream.

All praises are due to Allah who has taken away discomfort from me and granted me relief.

O Allah, You have made my body beautiful, so beautify my character also.

All praises are due to Allah who provided us with food and drink and made us believers.

O Allah, quench us, O Allah, bless us with rainfall.

O Allah, I seek refuge with You from a heart that knows no humility, from a soul that is never satisfied, from the knowledge that is of no use and from a prayer that is not answered.

A Kind Neighbour

Hibah Hassan

The Husseins were not only a very close-knit family, but were also very good friends with the people in their neighbourhood, such as the Khan family who lived to their right. However, the house on their left had been empty with a 'For Sale' signpost for as long as the Husseins could remember.

One Monday evening, when the children were returning from the park with the Khan children, Hamza noticed that the house next to theirs looked different. The old, dirty 'For Sale' sign had been replaced with a new 'Sold' sign!

They torpedoed through the front door to find Mum and all started speaking excitedly at once. Mum, in her usual calm way, handed each of the children a glass of milk and a cookie and said, "Yes, I saw it too, I'm glad that we will have some new neighbours! Once they have settled down, we can welcome them into our neighbourhood."

Over the next week, the children noticed a large moving van unloading furniture into the house.On Thursday, Fatima saw a car parking by the house and filled with excitement, called for her brothers and sister, " A'ISHA, HAMZA, ALI! The new neighbours are here!"

The children sped downstairs and were just about to open the front door when Mum stopped them, "Children, give them some time to relax, you can say hello tomorrow afternoon." After some protest, the children reluctantly went back upstairs and went to bed early, impatient for the next day.

Unkind Neighbour

While living in Makkah, one of Prophet Muhammad's ﷺ neighbour and his wife were very unkind to the Prophet. A surah was revealed mentioning the punishment for the couple.
What is the name of the Surah?

a. Al-Fil
b. Al- Masad
c. Al- Maun

Answer: b

Hadith

He is not a believer who has a square meal while his neighbour starves.

Ibn Majah

The next afternoon, the Husseins went to meet the new neighbours. A'isha rung the doorbell and a tall man with brown hair opened the door. Ali, excitedly blurted out, "Hello, I'm Ali, do you have anyone my size?" The man, very puzzled, looked at Ali and then at Ali's mother who said, "Assalamualykum, may peace be with you, we are your neighbours, the Husseins. Sorry about my son, he just wants to know if you have any children his age."

"Walaiykum assalam, yes, I'm Tariq Rehman, and yes… we have children." he paused and then called loudly to his children, "Ayan, Zuha, come here!" Two children came pounding down the stairs, both smiling. Fatima, A'isha, Ali and Hamza introduced themselves, Hamza gave them the cookies and Little Ali let them know that he was disappointed that Ayan was 14 and Zuha was 12.

After chatting about their new house, the Hussein children were about to leave and Ayan said, "We're having a welcome party tomorrow with lots of music, maybe you can come along as well!" Fatima, not sure what to say, replied "Uh, yeah... we'll ask Mum.'

The next evening, after the family had prayed Maghrib (evening), loud music blared in through their windows, music so sudden and loud that it upset little Ali. Ali's father comforted him with the ideas that the music would end in a few minutes. But fifteen minutes later, the music had not stop, in fact it just seemed to be louder.

The children patiently waited for the music to stop, but it didn't cease and played at full blast throughout dinner. Their father then went to watch the news and had to turn the volume up to hear it and when the family prayed Isha (night) together, they could hardly hear their father.

At bedtime, the children's father tucked them in and kissed them goodnight, but Ali couldn't sleep, he lay in bed, tossing and turning. At nine thirty, there was a loud "BANG!", and for the second time that day, Ali burst into tears. Throughout the night, there were loud noises and cheers that echoed throughout the street. Patiently, the parents ignored the music and tried to sleep, and around one in the morning, Mrs. Hussein was grateful to hear the music stop. The street was serene and silent.

The next day, when the children complained to Mum, she said, "Listen children, let's sort this problem out calmly and nicely, in the way that the Prophet would have… Did you know that since the Prophet Muhammad ﷺ was spreading Islam, the Arabs felt threatened by his new teachings, and they harassed the Prophet and were unkind to him. Even the Prophet's uncle, Abu Lahab, who was the Prophets neighbour; he and his wife both abused the Prophet verbally and physically. '

But the Prophet was always very kind and gentle with his neighbours. When one of the Prophet's companions asked him what it meant to be a good neighbour, the Prophet Muhammad ﷺ said that to be a good neighbour, you should helps those living around you if they need it. For example, if they need to borrow some money, you should help them out. The Prophet also told his people that you should visit your neighbours if they are sick or in some trouble.

Although the people of Makkah were not kind towards our Prophet, he still told people that you should offer your neighbours fruit and that you should congratulate them if anything good happens to them. We should follow his example and try to be kind to our neighbours as well."

She smiled and continued," Being a good neighbour is part of being a Muslim. In many cities today, people don't even know who lives next door – isn't that a shame?"

Abu Ayyub Ansari

Khalid bin Zaid, better known as Abu Ayyub Ansari in Islamic history, was one of the citizens of Madinah who embraced Islam early on. On his first arrival to Madinah, the Prophet stayed at Abu Ayyub Ansari's house. He made the Prophet's stay very comfortable. The Prophet stayed with Abu Ayyub and his family for about a month.

Worship God: and do not associate partners with Him. Be good to your parents, to relatives, to orphans, to the needy, and the neighbour who is a kinsman, and the neighbour who is not related to you and your companions and the wayfarers and those whom you rightfully possess. God does not like arrogant, boastful people.

Al-Nisa' 4:36

Little Ali nodded and asked, "But what can we do?"

"Well," said Mum, "We can either go to their house or ask them to please turn the volume down next time… Maybe we can take some cake with us. Or we can just ignore the problem." The children thought for a moment and said "The first one! That's a good idea!"

"Good choice children, you know that the Prophet encouraged people to give gifts to their neighbours. When the Prophet's wife A'isha asked whom she should send her gifts to, he replied, 'To the one whose door is closest to yours.' Islam tells us to take care of all our neighbours."

So the next day, the children took some cake to the neighbours, Mr and Mrs Rehman felt ashamed that their loud music had disturbed them and sincerely apologised. Fatima, Hamza, A'isha and Ali were very happy that their plan had worked and they never forgot the hadith about gifts.

A couple of days later, on a sunny afternoon, the doorbell rang and Fatima ran to answer it. There stood Ayan and Zuha with a plate of brownies, and a card that said 'We're sorry!' Ayan and Zuha thanked Fatima for teaching them such an important lesson, and from that day on, the two families were great friends and I'm sure they always will be!

A Simple Man

Hibah Hassan

Mum and Dad were returning from parents evening at the children's school. The children's teachers had been very happy with the children and had praised them a lot.

"Assalamu Alaykum, we are home!" called Mum as she entered the house. Fatima, Hamza and A'isha came thundering down the steps and little Ali followed them. "Wa Alaykumus-Salam." They said in unison, and they all started speaking at once. "Mum, what did my teacher say about me?" asked Fatima. "Dad, did my teacher say I was good?" asked Hamza. "Did they say I was naughty or not?" demanded Ali. "Did she show you my English poem?" asked A'isha.

Dad laughed, "Come here," he said, "Let's all go and sit down in the living room and we'll tell you what your teachers said." In the living room, Mum explained how delighted she was to hear so many good things about her children. She told each child what their teachers had said. Then Dad said, "As a reward, I will give each of you five pounds to spend when we go to the mall this evening." The children grinned; five pounds was a lot of money for them, they would be careful to spend it well.

Dad handed A'isha and Hamza five shiny pound coins and gave Fatima a crisp note, then he looked at Ali. "Do you want five pounds as well

Simple Living

Prophet Muhammad ﷺ despite his responsibilities as a prophet, a teacher, a statesman, and a judge, led a very simple life. He used to milk his goat, mend his clothes, repair his shoes, help with the household work. His house was made of unbaked clay and roof from the palm leaves. Which mosque was next to Prophet's house?

a. Masjid Al Haram
b. Masjid Al Aqsa
c. Masjid Al Nabawi

Answer: c

Hadith

Before entering someone's house, one should seek permission. One should return, if permission is not granted.

Abu Dawud

Ali?" he asked kindly. Ali scratched his head and thought, "No. I don't want just five pounds. I want fifty pence. Fifty pence is a lot more money than five pounds," he said. Fatima laughed and tried to explain, "No Ali, five pounds is more than fifty pence. Five pounds is five hundred pence!" But Ali just shook his head, "Five is not the same as five hundred! Five is the same as five, and fifty is more than five." He said impatiently, "Your teacher told Mum that you are good at math Fatima, but I do not think that you are too smart, you don't know that fifty is more than five!" he exclaimed.

Sensing that an argument was about to start, Mum stepped into the conversation. "Okay, okay. That's enough now. Ali can have fifty pence if he wants to; he has been helping me a lot around the house." Ali nodded.

"Fatima, A'isha and Hamza, why don't you all go upstairs and play?"

At five o' clock, after they had had tea, the family set off to the mall. At the mall, they first did some grocery shopping and then started walking to the toyshop. On the way to there, they passed many clothes and shoe shops. The children looked into the windows with awe. Fatima said that she wished that she had that beautiful pink shirt, A'isha asked Dad if he would buy her some new 'light up' trainers, Hamza told Mum that he would really love to have that spider man cap, and little Ali plodded along silently, tightly clenching his new fifty pence coin. Fatima then stopped her Mum in front of one of the clothes shop.

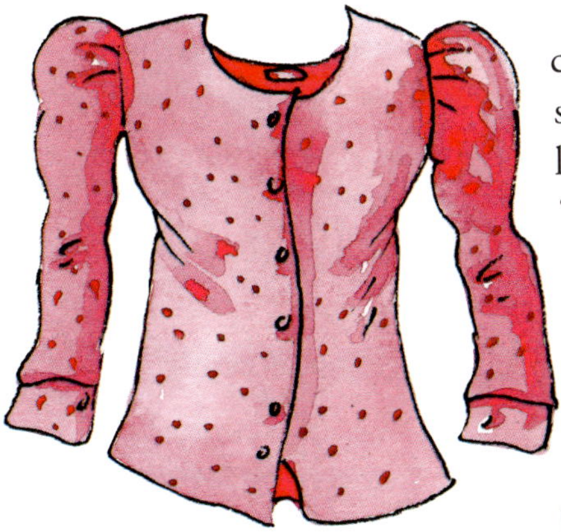

"Mum," she said, "See that orange jumper in the right corner? Farida in my classmate has one of them, and she says it's the most comfortable jumper in the world!" Mum looked at the jumper, "Well, it is quite pretty," she said. "But Fatima, didn't I buy you a red jumper last week? Why do you need another one?" Fatima sighed quietly, "I guess I don't really need it…" Dad nodded and said, "You know we are responsible for everything we do and all the money we spend. Did you know that even though the Prophet Muhammad ﷺ was such a great leader, he always led a simple life? He was never greedy and ate very little and only simple food. Some days, he would eat and drink nothing but a few dates and some water."

Hamza gasped, "Didn't the Prophet like eating milk and biscuits?"

Dad laughed, 'The Prophet loved milk, but I'm not sure about biscuits. He spent more money on gifts and charity rather than on himself. He had very few luxuries, he slept on a thin mat during the night, and he would sit on that same mat during the day. He rarely had more than two sets of clothes, and he washed his clothes himself. He lived like an ordinary man, even though the riches of many empires were flowing into his city."

"Wow!" said Fatima, "He hardly had anything! Only two sets of clothes! Imagine wearing the same thing every day! I have so many shirts and so many trousers already."

Dad smiled and Fatima realized what she was saying. She smiled sheepishly, "It looks like I don't really need that orange jumper."

"And I don't need those light up trainers." said A'isha. "Or the spider man cap" agreed Hamza.

The children all looked at Ali, waiting for him to say something. "But I need my fifty pence!" he said. They all laughed and little Ali grinned. A'isha spotted the toyshop and she, Fatima and Ali ran ahead. Hamza hung back with his parents.

"Why aren't you running to the toy shop?" Mum asked Hamza. Hamza replied, "Because I'm not going to buy anything, I do not have any money." "Hamza," said Mum gently, "What happened to the five pounds Dad gave you? Did you lose them?"

"No," said Hamza, "My money is at home in my piggy bank, my friend Mustafa said that he had been saving his money, and he hadn't bought anything for a whole year!

> Believers, give charitably from the good things which you have earned and what We produce for you from the earth; not worthless things which you yourselves would only reluctantly accept. Know that God is self-sufficient and praiseworthy.
>
> *Al- Baqarah 2:267*

And now he has thirty pounds!" Hamza's eyes grew wide in admiration. "So I have decided to also save my money," he announced. Hamza's parents raised their eyebrows, but did not say anything as they walked into the shop.

One of their close friends, 'Aunty Sarah' was working in the toyshop. Aunty Sarah was not really their Aunt, but the children loved her so much, they called her that. Hamza was the first one to spot Aunty Sarah at the counter. He ran up to her. "Assalamu Alaykum Aunty Sarah!" he exclaimed happily.

"Wa Alaykumus-Salam Hamza! How are you?" she replied.

"I am fine, *Alhamdulillah*. Aunty, have you seen A'isha, Fatima and Ali yet?" Aunty Sarah shook her head. "No, I haven't, but I'm sure I will see them in a while when they come to pay for their toys." Hamza nodded and then ran off to find his family. Half an hour later, the Hussein family gathered around the tills to pay for everything. A'isha went first. She had bought a lovely jigsaw puzzle, and it cost exactly five pounds. Next came Fatima. She had bought some new paints and a paintbrush which also cost five pounds. Both of the sisters were delighted to see Aunty Sarah. Ali had picked out a little deep blue teddy bear. The teddy bear cost one pound fifty. Aunty Sarah scanned the bear and Ali gave his fifty pence coin to Aunty Sarah. "But Ali," said Aunt Sarah, "You do not have enough money for the teddy bear." "Oh…" Said Ali, "The toyshop owner won't mind. He is a very rich man!" Aunt Sarah smiled kindly, "How do you know he is a rich man, Ali?" she asked. "Well, A'isha gave him five pounds and Fatima gave him five pounds and I gave him fifty! That's

a lot! He is very very rich!" Aunt Sarah smiled again and said, "Yes Ali, he must be rich, but we should always pay the right price for anything we buy." Aunt Sarah opened up her purse and put a small one pound coin into the cash desk. She gave Ali the receipt, and he hugged her, said "thank you" and ran away. Aunt Sarah then noticed Hamza looking at one of the action men. "Hamza," she said, "Haven't you decided what to buy yet?" Hamza shook his head and told Aunt Sarah his plan to get rich. Aunt Sarah then said, "Hamza, what will you do with all of that money?" Hamza thought for a moment and then shrugged his shoulders, "I'm not sure," he replied.

"The Prophet did not have much interest in money and he said, 'Miserable are those people who adore the dinar.' What he meant is that you should not always run after money, and keep collecting it. It is good to save for a good reason sometimes, but it's more important to use your money sensibly on your needs and, most important, on others."

Hamza nodded, "Yes there are more important things than money, like your family, and your friends."

"And your toys?" added Aunty Sarah.

"Thank you, Aunty, thank you for telling me such an important story," said Hamza. "I know what to do now." And he ran off to his parents. He borrowed five pounds from Dad, bought a book for 3 pounds and, when he got home, he opened his piggy bank and paid Dad back. Now he had two pounds left over. "I will save a little bit of money," said Hamza, and he dropped one of the two-pound coins into his piggy bank. But then he remembered Aunty Sarah telling him about the Prophet's generosity. He found lots of five and ten pence coins in his piggy bank. He picked up his two pounds, scooped up the various pieces of change in his hands and ran to Dad.

Uthman Ibn Affan

Uthman ibn Affan, accepted Islam in the very early days of Islam. He came to be known as 'Uthman Ghani' (Uthman the Rich). Uthman received a formal education and was one of the few people in Makkah who could read and write. The Prophet Muhammad ﷺ once said, "Uthman is the most modest of my Companions!" Uthman also developed a custom to free slaves every Friday, he looked after the widows and orphans, and gave a lot in unlimited charity.

> Who will offer God a generous loan? He will double it for him and give him a rich reward.
>
> *Al-Hadid 57:11*

"Dad! Dad! Aunty Sarah told me a very nice story about how the Prophet did not care a lot about money, and how he didn't save it all up. Saving is a good thing, but you should not hoard up all of your money. So I want to give this money to charity." Dad hugged Hamza and took the coins.

A Sincere Companion

Sarah Ali

The holidays were over and school had started again. Fatima could not control her excitement; she was actually starting Year 7 now! Everything was going to be different! Of course, there would be more homework, heavier books, and different rules, but she couldn't stop thinking about how much fun she would have with her best friend, Kinza.

Kinza was a great friend and she always advised Fatima about her religion. As Kinza stepped on to the bus, she gave Fatima a warm smile.

"Assalamu Alaykum, Fatima! How were your holidays?" inquired Kinza, excitedly. The girls sat side-by-side and proceeded to tell each other about their vacations.

The first month of school had gone by. Fatima and Kinza had met many new girls from different countries around the world. Some of them were very popular, such as Saima, who was very tall, pretty, and fun to be around with. She told funny jokes and everyone wanted to be her friend. But soon enough, they discovered that Saima wasn't all that she appeared to be. In fact, she was often heard gossiping and back-biting. She could also be very mean to some of the shy girls, she laughed and mocked their timidity. Fatima and Kinza could not stand Saima being a bully, and wanted to teach her about treating others with kindness, love and care.

One of Saima's victims was a girl called Diana. Fatima and Kinza knew that Muslims should always be courteous and polite to everyone, regardless of race and religion. One day, Kinza had had enough of Saima's attitude, and so, while Saima was busy laughing at Diana's hairstyle, she confronted her.

Migration to Madinah

When the Makkans hatched a plot to kill the Prophet Muhammad ﷺ, he left the city for Madinah. Who was the companion who accompanied the Prophet during the migration?

a. Abu Bakr
b. Umar Ibn Al Kattab
c. Uthman ibn Uffan

Answer: a

Hadith

Save yourselves from envy. For envy eats up virtues as fire eats up wood.

Abu Dawud

"Saima, how would you feel if someone treated you like this? Why do you keep hurting people?" Kinza shook her head in dismay. Fatima gave Saima a reproachful glance and the two walked away with Diana. No one had ever confronted Saima in such a manner before.

Diana was thankful to the two friends who had stood up for her and afterwards tentatively asked, "Kinza, Fatima, why did you stick up for me when I was being bullied by Saima?"

Fatima and Kinza smiled, and Kinza started with "Our religion, Islam, tells us that we must be kind and caring towards everyone. God loves those who care for others and will reward them."

"Oh my, I never knew that! Thanks for explaining," Diana said. She now understood that Islam was a peaceful religion which taught kindness and care for all individuals. The three girls then went to the Gymnasium for their P.E. lesson.

The P.E. teacher informed everyone about netball try-outs after school. "Hmm, I wonder if I can join in. It might be good fun, and besides, I'm not that bad at netball," said Fatima to Kinza, who simply shrugged and replied, "You can go, but I'm not coming. I'm not interested in netball."

Heading to the gym at break time, Fatima encountered Saima. "Hi! Are you signing up as well?" Saima asked Fatima with a smile.

This friendly approach took Fatima aback. Why was Saima speaking to her so politely, especially after the whole Diana thing? "So, are you any good? Well, you must be better than me! I'm horrible at it, but I do have a passion for sports!" Saima laughed and Fatima smiled, puzzled.

A cheerful Saima and a suspicious Fatima chatted all the way back after signing up. Fatima was honestly surprised by Saima's kind attitude towards her. She wanted to tell Kinza about this, but wasn't entirely sure about her reaction, so she decided otherwise.

As the weeks went by, Saima and Fatima slowly got closer and closer. At first, playing netball without Kinza made Fatima lonely, but now, Saima had proved to be an excellent partner.

"Assalamu Alaykum, Kinza," Fatima greeted her best friend on the bus one morning. She wanted to tell her about Saima. "You know Kinza, Saima plays netball with me and she is actually quite nice! When it comes to picking partners, she always chooses me over her other friends. Do you think we should get to know her a bit better?" Fatima asked, brightly.

"Maybe…" Kinza hesitantly replied.

Kinza slowly noticed that Saima and Fatima were starting to spend more time together. She missed her best friend terribly and was afraid that she had changed under Saima's influence. Even though Saima was close to Fatima, she was still the same bully to the other girls. Though Fatima never took part in her mockery, she never really tried to stop Saima either. And so, Kinza realized she had to do something about this.

One afternoon, Kinza spoke to her best friend on the bus, starting with "I've noticed that you have been spending a lot of time with Saima, it's good that you have another friend but..."

Fatima tried to interrupt, but Kinza continued, "Before you say anything, I have something to tell you from what the Prophet said about friends. "A person is likely to follow the faith of his friend, so look whom you befriend." Please be careful if you are becoming friends with Saima. The Prophet also said, "The example of a good companion and a bad companion is like that of the seller of musk, and the one who

Abu Bakr

Abu Bakr is respected as one of the most sincere companion of the Prophet Muhammad ﷺ.
When the Prophet received the first revelation from Allah and when he was taken to the Heavens (*Al-Mi'raj*), Abu Bakr believed the Prophet and stood by him. Thus, he earned the title of 'al-Siddiq', which means a very strong and honest friend. The Prophet once said, "No one has been a better companion to me than Abu Bakr."

> Help one another in goodness and in piety. Do not help one another in sin and transgression. Fear God! God is severe in punishment.
>
> *Al- Maidah 5:2*

blows the blacksmith's bellows. So, as for the seller of musk, then either he will grant you some, or you buy some from him, or at least you enjoy a pleasant smell from him. As for the one who blows the blacksmith's bellows, then either he will burn your clothes or you will get an offensive smell from him." This hadith says that you can never gain anything from bad company. They will only hurt and harm you in the long run."

Fatima did not like Kinza's seemingly bold lecture and from that day on, she avoided her; though in her heart she knew that Kinza was right, and she herself was disturbed by Saima's wrong behaviour.

The next day, Saima was bullying a new girl, Kelly. Instead of watching like a bystander, Fatima called, "Saima, come on. Let's go eat." Slowly, she was trying to stop Saima from bullying altogether.

It was the last week of term and the class was having their math's assessment.

"You may begin the test."

Papers were turned and pens were heard. Fatima had already turned to the second page while Saima, who was next to her, hadn't even started. Mrs Richards glared at her until she began her test.

"Pssst!" Saima's whispers interrupted Fatima's calculations. She was pointing at a question. Fatima was afraid. What should she do?

Without thinking, Fatima quickly turned to Question 4 and said,

"8x + 30 -..."

She shut her mouth as

Mrs Richards stormed right up to their desks.

Without a word, she snatched their papers as the entire class stared in shock at Fatima, who was almost in tears. Why had she done something so stupid? She realized that the only one that could help her now was Allah. She turned to her Lord with a sincere heart and begged Him to help her out of the situation. Both girls were asked to stay in the classroom.

"Right! This is unacceptable behaviour. I want you to take the responsibility and tell me who copied who!" Mrs Richards demanded firmly.

But before Fatima could open her mouth, Saima's finger pointed at her in accusation, stunning Fatima. "She cheated on me! She did it! Honestly!" Saima hysterically cried, pointing at her friend.

To everyone's surprise Kinza knocked and entered the room, "Mrs Richards, I have a suggestion for you," not pausing for an answer, "I think you should check the question they cheated on, then ask them a similar question orally."

Mrs Richards agreed to this idea and after quizzing both of the girls privately, it was clear that Fatima was innocent. Upon this assertion, Saima failed the assignment and her parents were called.

Fatima thanked Allah repeatedly for saving her from a desperate situation.

Fatima brought a present for Kinza and apologized sincerely for ignoring her earlier. Kinza smiled and hugged her friend with affection. Her best friend was back! But Fatima still had one question left…

"How come you stood up for me when I was ignoring you?"

Kinza smiled and replied, "Because I still care about you. I learnt this from the greatest role model of all time, the Prophet Muhammad ﷺ." Fatima looked confused.

"He had many companions, who all loved him dearly and were willing to die for him. Have you ever thought about it, Fatima, how could so many people love our Prophet to the extent that they put their lives in danger?" Kinza continued.

> You have indeed in the Prophet of God a good example for those of you who look to God and the Last Day, and remember God always.
>
> *Al- Ahzab 33:21*

Fatima was surprised, as she had never thought about it like that. Kinza added, "At the time of the migration to Madinah, Ali ibn Abi Talib slept on the Prophet's bed to help the Prophet and Abu Bakr to leave in the darkness of the night. Why would he do that? Wasn't it a big risk to his life? First of all, Ali had strong faith in Allah and His Prophet, and believed that everything happens by Allah's will. He had also seen the Prophet's love and care for all his companions. Ali and all his other companions were as sincere to the Prophet as the Prophet was to them."

Fatima was impressed with Kinza's way of thinking. Agreeing with her, she said, "True, Kinza, the Prophet Muhammad ﷺ lived all his life caring for, and teaching his companions to build a society based on faith and brotherhood."

"That's right, the Prophet always encouraged his companions to show that they loved and cared for others."

"I knew all of this. but never thought that we could follow the Prophet in our friendships too.

I can clearly see now how he earned the love of his companions," added Fatima in awe.

"Yes, these all are the qualities of a great friend; care, compassion and above all, forgiveness." Kinza concluded smiling.

The girls hugged each other once again, both feeling grateful to Allah for giving them such a beautiful friendship.

A Brilliant Teacher

Ameena Golding

"Maybe just a touch more... Yes, perfect!" said A'isha to herself, as she finished applying some eyeshadow. Fatima walked in.

"Hey Fatima," said A'isha, still preoccupied with putting on her makeup. "Hay is for horses," laughed Fatima. "I think the word you are looking for is 'Assalamu Alaykum'."

"Oh yeah, sorry, I meant Assalamu Alaykum." Fatima was thirteen, prayed five times a day and read the Quran a lot. On the other hand, A'isha, who was ten, often forgot to pray and this would frustrate Fatima. A'isha would focus on applying her makeup, trying different hairstyles, or remembering when the next designer handbags would go on sale.

"A'isha, do you really need to wear that much make-up?" asked Fatima, gazing at her in distaste. Fatima didn't wear a lot of make-up, because she knew it was important in Islam for women to be modest in their appearance.

"Of course I need to wear all this makeup. I need to keep up with the latest fashion trends, or else people at school will start to think I'm not cool, duh!" said A'isha, starting to get frustrated by her sister's grouchy remarks. "Gosh, you're so boring, Fatima. When was the last time you dressed up, or carried a trendy handbag? All you do is wear your frumpy trousers and long tops! You're just jealous because I'm so much cooler than you." There was a long silence.

"You know what? I don't know why I even bother trying to make you see the errors of your ways, A'isha. You're never going to change! Go on, wear all those expensive clothes and forget your religion! SEE IF I CARE! I HATE BEING YOUR

The King of Rome

In the seventh Hijri, the Prophet Muhammad ﷺ addressed letters to the kings of Persia, Yeman, Ethiopia, Egypt and others urging them to embrace Islam. Negus, the King of Ethiopia embraced Islam. Name the Roman Emperor who was greatly influenced by the Prophet Muhammad's teachings but could not embrace Islam due to his love of the throne and crown and the opposition from courtiers.

a. Hurmuz
b. Hauza bin Ali
c. Hercules Caesar

Answer: c

Hadith

The strong man is not the one who is good at wrestling, but the one who controls himself in a fit of rage.

Bukhari & Muslim

SISTER!" shouted Fatima, banging the door shut. She retreated to her own room and suddenly felt guilty for shouting at her younger sister.

"Fatima?" called Dad, knocking at the bedroom door. "Fatima dear, what's going on?" Fatima opened the door and explained how A'isha had been neglecting her prayers and Quran studies, because she was too busy spending time on clothes and other material things.

"Dear, I can see you are concerned. So am I, but shouting doesn't resolve anything," said Dad, calming Fatima down.

"I know, I shouldn't have shouted. I let my anger get the better of me," said Fatima.

"You know, the Prophet Muhammad ﷺ was a teacher, " said Dad. "Really?" replied Fatima, surprised. "Yes! Didn't he teach people about Islam throughout his life?" said Dad.

"Oh yeah, of course!" exclaimed Fatima. Dad continued: "You know, Fatima in teachers' training courses we were taught to be clear and direct with our students, to add humour and use parables. Children understand more if they know how to apply the knowledge they acquire," said Dad. "The Prophet Muhammad ﷺ was always direct and clear in his teachings. He explained things very clearly to his companions: 'Every religion has a distinctive quality and the distinctive quality of Islam is modesty.' Similarly, about manners, he said, 'The best of you are those who possess the best of manners.' He used to ask his companions questions and sometime used parables to explain the teachings of Islam, e.g. when he was teaching some companions about the virtues of Wudu, the Prophet asked them, "Do you think any dirt will remain on a person if he has a river by his house and he washes himself in it five times a day?", and the companions replied, "No." He then said "This is what happens when you perform wudu five times a day and pray."

"That's a nice way Dad! We always enjoy the classes where teachers are relaxed and humorous. I can see how the Prophet's way of teaching transformed the worst nation into the best of the nations. Thanks Dad for showing me the right way to correct my sister." Dad smiled, "You are most welcome, Fatima."

It was Friday morning, and the girls were getting ready for school. A'isha stared into her bowl of cornflakes, stirring the milk slowly and aimlessly.

"A'isha, are you actually going to eat your breakfast or just stare at it?" called Mum. "I don't really feel like eating anything," replied A'isha quietly. Mum realized something was wrong, "Is this about your little argument with Fatima yesterday?"

"I... I just don't really know. I mean, I thought I was doing the right thing by making myself popular. The most important thing is to have lots of friends, right? If I'm popular then I'll surely do well in life!" said A'isha, though not entirely convinced, "What's wrong with having lots of clothes and make-up?"

"Assalamu Alaykum A'isha," said Fatima, as she opened the door to the kitchen. "Wa Alaykumus-Salam," replied A'isha quietly.

"A'isha, I am sorry for shouting at you like that. I shouldn't have gotten so angry," said Fatima, feeling ashamed.

"It's okay. I just don't see why I shouldn't wear all these designer clothes and makeup..." A'isha trailed off.

Fatima, rather than getting angry, spoke gently, "A'isha, I want to tell you a story, One day, the Prophet Muhammad ﷺ returned from a journey and went to visit his loving daughter Fatima, when he reached her house, he didn't enter, but turned back. Ali was told about this and he came to the Prophet and inquired about it. The Prophet replied, "I saw a multi- coloured curtain on your door and I am not interested in worldly things." Ali told Fatima

A'isha Siddiqa

One of the Prophet Muhammad's wives, A'isha Siddiqa, was the daughter of Abu Bakr Siddiq, the first caliph of Islam. A'isha was blessed with an extraordinary intelligence. A'isha served as a teacher of the teachers after the Prophet. She would correct those teaching in the Prophet's mosque and answer those who came to her seeking rulings, advice and opinions. At the time of *'Hajjat al-Wida'* (the Farewell Hajj) the Prophet had said, "Learn some of your 'deen' (faith) from this red-haired lady," meaning A'isha.

Greed for more and more distracted you [from God] till you reached the grave. But you will soon come to know. But you will soon come to know. Indeed, were you to know the truth with certainty, you would see the fire of Hell. You would see it with the eye of certainty. Then on that Day you shall be questioned about your worldly favours.

Al- Takathur 102:1-8

about this and Fatima said, "I am ready to dispense with it as he suggests." The Prophet suggested we should give it in charity to needy people." And Fatima did so." A'isha listened intently. "So you see A'isha, we shouldn't get too attached to material things... like designer handbags. We should focus on doing good and look forward to the pleasures of the next life," ended Fatima.

"Wow, I didn't know that. Sorry Fatima, I really should have listened to you," said A'isha in an apologetic tone.

"It's okay to wear a bit of makeup, or to carry a nice bag, but don't waste your time and money on it so much that you forget what really matters in life, like being a good person and a better Muslim," said Fatima. "Yeah, you're right, thanks," agreed A'isha.

The two girls smiled. "Now are you ready to go to school?" asked Fatima. "Wait, there's just one quick thing I have to do," said A'isha, running upstairs. Five minutes later, she came downstairs carrying a sack full of bags. She had also removed some of her make-up.

"Um A'isha, the point of that story was that you would carry fewer bags, not more," said Fatima, desperately trying not to raise her voice. "Oh no, Fatima, these bags aren't for me. I'm taking them to the charity shop on the way to school," said A'isha. Fatima looked surprised.

"Oh, well done!" she said, as she smiled at her younger sister.

A'isha walked into the cafeteria. She could see her friends, Lamiya and Ruhina sitting at the table by the window. A'isha waved at them eagerly from the queue. "Ruhina, is that really A'isha?" whispered Lamiya in a surprised tone. "Yeah, I think that's her. Doesn't she look different without the make-up?" replied Ruhina.

"I know, right? She used to be so cool! What has happened to her now? Maybe if we go on hanging out with her, we might not stay popular any more…" said Lamiya, worried about what others would think of her. "Quickly, she's coming over now. Let's just pretend that we have to go to history class, or something," whispered Ruhina.

"Assalamu Alaykum, Lamiya and Ruhina!" exclaimed A'isha, joining them at the table.

"Uh, hey A'isha," said Lamiya, "Listen, we really have to go to history class. Um, talk to you later." Ruhina and Lamiya quickly walked off. "But it's still lunch time! Classes don't start for another half an hour!" A'isha called after them. A'isha was upset. She had followed her sister's advice and look what had happened – she not only became unpopular but her two best friends had ditched her! She tried to use her math folder as a shield so that no one could see her crying. From the corner of her tear-filled eyes, she could see Fatima walking over towards her.

"A'isha, are you OK? What's wrong?" exclaimed Fatima.

"Everything. Everything's wrong, Fatima," wailed A'isha, "I tried so hard to follow your advice but now my friends have left me and I'm not popular anymore."

"A'isha, it's OK, listen to me," began Fatima, hugging her sister and trying to comfort her. "Life isn't all about being popular. It's about doing good deeds and pleasing Allah. Remember, the Prophet Muhammad ﷺ said, 'Modesty is a part of faith, and faith leads to heaven; while vulgarity leads to hardness of heart and hardness of heart leads to Hell'. You're doing the right thing."

"Yeah, I know, but…" Before A'isha could say anything else, Anisah, one of the most popular girls in school walked up to A'isha. "Oh hey, loser!" jeered Anisah, sticking her tongue out at A'isha, who was so angry that she would have strode over to Anisah and hurt her, if it weren't for Fatima holding her back and saying "A'isha, just ignore them. You're doing the right thing and Allah

Our Lord ! we have wronged our souls:
if You do not forgive us and have mercy on us,
we shall be among the lost.
Al-Araf 7:23

will reward you, Insha'Allah." A'isha felt like she had to say something - she had to stick up for herself. "Anisah, do you even know that the Prophet Muhammad ﷺ advised Muslim women to always be modest in their appearance? Life isn't all about clothes and fashion. It's about being a good person and doing good deeds to please Allah. So I'm not going to listen to your teasing!" exclaimed A'isha. Anisah was taken aback by A'isha's sudden confidence and belief in what she was saying. "Wait, so the Prophet Muhammad ﷺ advised women to dress modestly?" said Anisah looking shocked, "I didn't know that." she trailed off. "Yes, he did. Someone once told me a story-" began A'isha, glancing at Fatima, "-a true story. It was about the Prophet Muhammad ﷺ and his beloved daughter Fatima." A'isha then began to tell Anisah, and a few other girls who had gathered round.

"Um, thanks for telling me that, A'isha. I didn't know that," said Anisah quietly, looking down at the floor in sheer embarrassment. Fatima looked at A'isha, feeling happy about the way her younger sister had handled the situation, maintaining her poise and calm. "I'm sorry A'isha for being so mean and treating you in such a way. You really have inspired me by telling that story. Really, I had no idea that Muslim women are supposed to be modest. I guess we all learn something new every day," said Anisah with a little nervous laugh. "It's okay, " replied A'isha, smiling.

"Hey, you know what we should do?" said Anisah, "we should set up a club for Muslim girls, where they can come and get advice on similar issues. I didn't know all this, and I'm sure there are loads of Muslim girls in this school who would be interested in learning about Islam." "That's a great idea Anisah!" replied A'isha.

An Ambitious Traveller

Umema Imran

"Holiday!" Hamza screamed in delight as he ran inside the house after school.

His twin sister A'isha followed him, skipping happily. Mrs. Hussein smiled at the reaction of her children. The kids were extremely happy because it was a long weekend. "Assalamu Alaykum," Mum called loudly from the living room. In their excitement, they had forgotten to say Salam to their Mum. "Wa Alaykumus-Salam, Mum," the three said in unison, still jumping up and down. She grinned as the sound of the door opening reached her ears.

"Assalamu Alaykum! What's all the commotion about?" Dad asked as he entered the very hyper scene.

"Wa Alaykumus-Salam, Dad. You're home early?" Fatima asked emerging from the kitchen.

"Well, we have some preparations to do. Are you all ready for the trip tomorrow?" He answered.

"What trip?" Hamza asked quizzically, finally stopping his happy screams.

"You didn't tell them, Sarah?" Mr Hussein turned to Mum.

"They got here five minutes ago and they've been like jumping beans ever since.

It's hard to get a word in," she explained.

"Well then," said Dad settling down on the sofa, "I guess I'll do the honours."

He turned to his expectant kids. "I thought that since recently both A'isha and Hamza have been studying about caves in school why don't we take a little road trip to the White Scar Cave."

The Holy Spirit

When the Prophet Muhammad ﷺ was 40 years of age, prophet hood was bestowed upon him. He was in the cave of Hira when an angel appeared before him and taught him the first five *ayahs* of Surah Al-Alaq. Name the angel who brought the revelation.

a. Jibril
b. Malik
c. Neither of the above

Answer: a

Hadith

Make things easy for people, do not make them hard for them.

Bukhari

"Cool!" said Hamza in awe, "Umm… what is that?"

"That's a cave, silly," Fatima explained, giggling, "And I've heard awesome things about it."

"Like what?" A'isha asked curiously, "It's not haunted, is it?"

"No, of course not!" said Fatima indignantly, "There's cool stuff in there. Like a rock that looks like a judge's head."

"Wow!" said Hamza, his eyes shining, "I definitely want to go there."

"Well then, its settled," said Dad happily, "InshaAllah, we're going to the White Scar Cave tomorrow!" And so the next day, the entire family took a road trip up to the caves. White Scar Cave was a lot of fun for everyone. They had never been to a cave like this before and were fascinated by all that they saw. The guide explained the wonders around them to the family. He showed them the witches' finger, which was a formation of rocks looking like long pointy fingers. A'isha shuddered when she saw them; they were slightly creepy. Suddenly someone cackled behind her. The frightened girl jumped a foot in the air and turned around to see her older sister laughing hysterically.

"Mum!" A'isha complained.

"Fatima, don't scare your little sister," said Mrs. Hussein reproachfully and Fatima giggled and apologized. The group moved on, touring the cave, seeing all the sights like the judge's head that Fatima had mentioned earlier. Mr. Hussein noticed that Hamza looked slightly uncomfortable.

When they got out, Mum suggested that they go sit in a field and have a picnic. Everyone was hungry by now and they eagerly munched on the sandwiches Mum had prepared and brought for them. Hamza wasn't talking much and ate his sandwich silently.

"What's up with you?" said Fatima, looking over.

"Nothing," said Hamza quietly.

"Did the cave scare you?" Dad asked gently, "You didn't look very happy."

"They were so dark and creepy…" Hamza confessed.

"But we are not in caves any more. So what's with the long face?" Fatima asked puzzled.

"Well I just remembered about the Prophet in the cave on his way to Madinah. He probably didn't have any light in the cave and he wasn't scared. And how am I supposed to follow the Prophets when I'm such a big chicken?" said Hamza sadly. Mum smiled at him. "Do you remember the entire incident?" she asked him.

"Umm... yeah, I guess," said Hamza, thinking it over, "The Prophet was with Abu Bakr on their way to Madinah. There were people from Makkah coming after them so they hid in a cave. Allah ordered a spider to make a web over the cave entrance so that when the people from Makkah reached the cave, they would assume that nobody was inside. So Allah saved the Prophet."

"Very good," said Mr Hussein encouragingly, "Do you know that there is very popular hadith about that incident?"

"What?" asked Hamza.

"When the Makkans were close to the cave, Abu Bakr was worried that they would be seen. The Prophet asked Abu Bakr 'What he thought of two people of whom Allah was the third,' Dad also told him an ayah in the Quran related to this incident, 'God did support him when those who denied the truth expelled him when the two of them were in cave, he (Muhammad) told his companion, 'Do not worry; for God is with us.'" (9: 40) "But what does that mean?" asked A'isha confused.

"It means that Abu Bakr shouldn't be scared since Allah was with them, and Allah protects whomever He wills. We should have faith in Allah," Mum explained.

"So..." Hamza began, understanding finally, "When I was in the cave I shouldn't have worried because I believe in Allah and He is always with me and He will protect me."

"Yes. But that doesn't mean that you should put yourself in danger, just for having fun," said Mum, clearing it up, "You can't just jump from a high place for fun, thinking that you can do whatever you want since Allah is watching over you. That would just be silly."

Ubadah Ibn Samit

Ubadah ibn Samit was among the early converts to Islam. He belonged to the Khazraj tribe of Madinah and was one of the twelve Madinites who had pledged allegiance to the Prophet at the First Pledge of Aqabah. Ubadah ibn Samit was one of those companions who travelled far and wide to spread Islam. Ubadah travelled to Syria and Palestine and taught people the Quran and hadith. He lived in Palestine and engaged himself in teaching the Quran and hadith"

> Read! In the name of your Lord, who created: created man from a clot [of blood]. Read! Your Lord is the Most Bountiful One who taught by the pen, taught man what he did not know.
> *Al-'Alaq 96:1-5*

"Do you feel better now?" Dad asked Hamza. He nodded in agreement.

"Sometimes people are so scared of going anywhere that they usually stay cooped up in one place for their whole life," said Dad talking to everyone now. "Even when it is very important for them, as when they should be acquiring knowledge or spreading the message of Islam."

"That sounds pretty boring," Fatima commented, "I mean there is so much to see and learn in the world." Dad nodded. "There is! The Prophet himself was a great traveller. He went to cities like Taif, Quba and, of course, Madinah to preach Islam."

"Wow," A'isha murmured.

"The Prophet was an ambitious traveller. He was not hesitant to travel to spread the message of Islam. Like the Hijrah was a great journey by the Muslims to find a safe city to live in and follow Islam," said Dad. "He didn't travel around to waste time. He went with a mission."

"Dad, is our trip to the cave a waste of time?"

"Well, we didn't come here unnecessarily, did we?" he replied. "We came here to learn about the caves and gain knowledge. That is a very good reason to travel."

The children were thinking over what Dad had said when their thoughts were interrupted by snoring sounds. They turned and found little Ali sleeping in Mum's lap. Everyone laughed.

"I think we should pack up and head back home," Dad suggested.

The children agreed and cleaned up their mess. Mum carried Ali to the car while Hamza and A'isha hauled the picnic basket together and they drove back home.

An Exemplary Leader

Umema Imran

Dinner at the Hussein family was a time when the whole family would sit together. Today was no different as the family began the meal together with the name of Allah.

Dad noticed that Fatima was sitting quietly and was not paying attention to the antics of her siblings.

"Fatima?" he asked, and she was jerked out of her thoughts, "Is something wrong?"

"No," Fatima shrugged, "Just some school stuff."

"Anything you need help with?" Mum asked, also looking over.

Fatima answered slowly, "Yeah... I guess so, there's this group project our class got for school," Fatima began explaining, "We were randomly sorted into groups and the teacher chose a leader for each team. But my partners had a problem with our leader and the teacher made me the group leader." Fatima looked desperately at her parents.

"You don't want to be the group leader?" Dad asked.

"No!" she exclaimed, "I'm so scared that I'm going to mess up everything, and my entire group will get a bad grade, all because of me. I will be a failure!" Fatima finished frantically.

The First Mosque

In the 6th Hijri the Prophet led a group of Muslims from Madinah to Makkah. On the way, they were stopped by a Makkan army commander. Both the parties signed a peace agreement? What was that?

a. The Peace Treaty of Hudaybiyyah
b. The Pact of Fudul
c. The Pact of Makkah

Answer: a

Mum looked slightly amused, "Oh honey, I think that you are making a mountain out of a molehill. You won't be a failure."

"Make a what out of a what?" A'isha asked confused.

"A mountain out of a molehill." Mum explained, "It means to make a bigger deal out of something than it really is."

Dad spoke, "You won't mess up anything. It's your first time to lead, it's natural to be nervous. Remember, there is always first time for everything

Hadith

Allah does not look at your body and face, rather, He looks at your heart.

Muslim

and what better time to learn how to lead than now?"

"But... how do I learn to be a good leader?" Fatima asked, confused.

"By the following the examples of the greatest leader of all time!" Dad said, and upon seeing the confused look on Fatima's face, he said, "The Prophet Muhammad ﷺ"

"Oh!" Fatima said, finally understanding.

"What are you so worried about?" Hamza asked his sister, "Being a leader is easy. All you have to do is sit and boss people around."

"Come to think of it, "Fatima said, thinking back, "The previous leader did put all the work on everyone else. She said her job was to supervise us."

"That's not fair for the rest of you" Mum added.

"Now, if she had followed the example of the Holy Prophet ﷺ , she would not have piled all the work on her team. She would have taken active part in the assignment, just like the Prophet ﷺ did. You all remember Masjid-un-Nabwi from when we went for Umrah, don't you?" Dad asked the children.

"I remember!" Ali spoke up excitedly, "It is a very big mosque."

"You're right Ali." Dad smiled, "Masjid-un-Nabwi is one of the earliest mosques built by Muslims in Madinah. It was a place where all the Muslims would gather and pray. People would study Islam there, and if there was a problem, it was brought to the Prophet in the mosque so he could make the correct and just decision. However, it was not as big and beautiful as it is today; back then it was a simple room with the roof made of mud, stones and palm leaves."

And you know all the Muslims along with Prophet Muhammad ﷺ worked together to built it." Dad added, "As the Prophet ﷺ was a leader, he could have easily told his followers to do all the work. His companions actually urged him not to take part, but the Prophet ﷺ did his equal share."

"Wow!" Hamza muttered.

"I know another incident like that." Fatima told Dad,

"During the Battle of Ahzab, a huge army of disbelievers was marching towards Madinah. One of the companions advised digging

a trench around Madinah to protect the city. The Prophet also took part in the digging. At that time, there was a drought in Madinah and there wasn't enough to eat. Once a companion of the Prophet ﷺ showed him the stones he had tied around his waist to overcome hunger and asked if the Prophet ﷺ had something to eat. The Prophet lifted his shirt and showed that he too had stones tied around his waist since he had nothing to eat for days as well."

"Very good, Fatima." Dad gave her a nod of approval, "You see how he led by example. Apart from that, a quality of a good leader is bravery. I know that you are scared about leading, but you should not let that stop you."

"Jazakallah Mum and Dad. Sometimes I never realize how many great examples we have from the life of the Prophet ﷺ ." Thanked Fatima

The next day at school, it was Fatima's group meeting, and the girls in her group were having a heated argument. Fatima tried to break it up.

"Listen." She said in a quiet voice but they ignored her. She considered calling the teacher for help, then remembered Dad's words from the previous night telling her how the Prophet ﷺ had been a strong leader.

"Girls!" she said loudly, breaking up the squabble, "Please stop fighting. We don't have time to waste. We can solve this maturely, without arguments."

The girls looked at her, surprised to see her speaking so strongly.

"I was thinking that Hafsah could draw some of the drawings, since she is good at art," Hafsah smiled, happily at Fatima's words, "And Maryam could design the computer presentation since she is probably the best." Maryam cheered up at her leaders compliment.

"What do you have in mind, Khadijah?" Fatima asked the previous leader.

"Pretty much what you said," Khadijah shrugged, "I think I should present the project to the class."

"That's a good idea, but that does not mean that you don't help us with the rest of the work." Maryam told her. Khadijah grumbled slightly but didn't challenge her.

Umm Sulaym

Umm Sulaym, mother of Anas ibn Malik, a famous Companion of the Prophet, was the first woman in Madinah to accept Islam. She was a role model for Muslim women because of her strong and uncompromising belief in Allah. She devoted herself and all her belongings to the service of Islam.

> It is by God's grace that you were gentle with them—for if you had been harsh and hard-hearted, they would surely have deserted you—so bear with them and pray for forgiveness for them. Take counsel with them in the conduct of affairs; then, when you have decided upon a course of action, place your trust in God: for God loves those who place their trust in Him.
>
> *Al-'Imran 3:159*

"So I guess that leaves me and you collecting the information," Fatima told Alisha who nodded, "So let's get to work."

Two week later, Fatima returned from school so happy that she was almost bouncing on the ground. "Assalamualykum Mum!" she said as the Mum opened the door.

"WalaikumAssalam, hey Fatima Masha Allah you look very happy" Mum said, "What's the good news?"

"My group got the highest marks in the class project!" Fatima exclaimed excitedly.

"Mash Allah! That's wonderful. The same project that you were leading, right?" Mum asked grinning.

"Yeah." Fatima replied.

"The same project you were worried you would fail and become a failure in life?"

"…Yeah." Fatima said laughing.

"Well that worked out well didn't it?" Mum asked, also laughing.

"Alhamdulillah. There were times when I was really confused as to what I should do, but then I remembered what you and Dad told me about the Prophet's leadership and then the answers became simple enough." Fatima explained.

"You must have seen that following the example of the Prophet makes our life easier as it teaches us many lessons." Mum said.

Fatima nodded. From her experience she could guarantee that the Sunnah of the Prophet ﷺ is the best example in any situation.

The Prophet as a Grandfather

Hibah Hassan

It was 10 o'clock in the morning and the Hussein family house was unusually quiet. Ali was at his friend's house and Fatima and her parents were attending a big lecture about the importance of reading Quran in their local community centre. The children's Grandmother was coming over to look after A'isha and Hamza who were too young and impatient for such an event. The twins were very fond of their grandmother and were looking forward to spending the day with her."

When the doorbell rang, their grandmother stood there smiling with her arms outstretched "Assalamualykum! How are you?"

"WalaikumAssalam Grandma! We are fine Alhamdulillah!" said the twins.

Grandmother walked into the living room and the twins sat down on her lap. Dad told grandmother that they would be back by one thirty and InshaAllah would have lunch together. They hugged the little ones and reminded them to behave and listen to their grandmother. A'isha and Hamza smiled demurely and nodded.

Grandma led the children to the living room and said, "So, what shall we do today?"

A'isha said, "Grandma, every Friday, our whole family goes to the mosque together to pray Jumaah, so can you take us today?"

"Of course, what a good idea A'isha! Your grandfather will also be at the mosque, we'll go at half past eleven."

The Divine Gift

In the eleventh year of prophethood, the Prophet Muhammad ﷺ was taken for Isra and Meraj (the Night Journey and the Ascent). The Angel Jibril took him from Makkah to al-Aqsa mosque at Jerusalem and from there to the seven heavens.

During this journey Allah gave him a divine gift. What was that?

a. Swam (fasting)
b. Salat (daily prayers)
c. Hajj (pilgrimage)

Answer: b

Hadith

If a young man honors an older man on account of his age, God appoints someone to show reverence to him in his old age.

Tirmidhi

They then went upstairs and played snakes and ladders, chess, snap and coloured in their colouring books. The twins were delighted to win every game they played; it seemed that their grandmother wasn't very good at board games! At eleven fifteen they all made Wudu and Hamza put on his small, white cap. A'isha put on her pale pink flowery headscarf and ran eagerly to her grandmother. "Grandma! Grandma, look at my scarf it has flowers just like yours!" Grandma smiled, "Yes it does, mashaAllah you and Hamza look very cute."

The children jumped into grandma's small blue car and grandma drove them to the mosque. They took off their shoes and Hamza, who spotted his grandfather amongst the other men, ran into the men's section. The Imam said the *khutba* and the *iqama* was called and everyone got into straight lines facing the Qibla, the imam raised his hands and said "*Allah hu akbar*" and the people followed. When the prayer was over they all got up and greeted each other.

Grandmother explained that the mosque was not only a place of prayer, it was the hub of the Muslim community, and where Muslims met each other, where Quran and Arabic lessons took place. She explained how during the prophet's time, although the mosque was very small, Muslims would come from afar to listen to the prophet who gave da'waah and told them about Islam.

Grandma then greeted all of the ladies and asked A'isha to tell her grandfather that they were ready to leave. A'isha went to the entrance of the men's section and scanned the room for Hamza or her Grandfather; she quickly found Hamza talking to his friends and saw her grandfather standing amongst a group of men. A'isha waved at Hamza and he came running over to her.

"Grandma told me to get Grandpa, but he is busy with his friends and the Imam.
I'm not sure if he will like being interrupted…"Hamza nodded, "Grandpa is very kind, but he might not like it if we disturb him. What do you think we should do A'isha?" A'isha shrugged her shoulders and said, "I don't know, let's go and tell Grandma that he is busy."

So the children ran into the ladies section to their Grandma and told her how Grandpa might not like to be

interrupted. “He might get angry with us...” trailed off Hamza.

“Oh children! Your grandfather would never be angry with you, just like the Prophet Muhammad ﷺ would not get angry with his grandchildren for such a thing. You know, one day, when the Prophet was leading prayer, his young grandchildren ran up to him in excitement. When the Prophet prostrated they started climbing onto his back!” Hamza and A’isha were astonished.

“The Prophet must have been very angry with them for jumping on his back and interrupting his prayer.” A’isha thought out loud.

Grandmother shook her head and carried on, “No dear, the prophet loved his grandchildren and all the children in general very much and did not want to spoil their fun, so do you know what he did? Instead of pushing the children off his back to continue with the prostration, he patiently waited until they had finished playing. When his grandchildren climbed off his back, the Prophet carried on with his prayer. At the end of the prayer, the people crowded around him asking many questions, “Oh Prophet of Allah, why did you stay so long in Prostration?” “Was Allah sending you a revelation?” “Did you forget that you were leading a prayer?”

The prophet looked at the bewildered people and picked his grandchildren both up and showed the people, “This is the reason why I stayed so long in prostration - they were playing on my back. I did not wish to spoil their fun”. He

Hassan and Hussein

Hassan and Hussein were the sons of Ali ibn Talib and Fatima Bint Muhammad. The Prophet Muhammad ﷺ visited his daughter often and would love to spend time with his grand children. The Prophet Muhammad ﷺ once said about his grandsons, “Hassan and Hussein are leaders of the youths in Paradise.”

> Lord, my bones have weakened and my head has turned white with age, but never, Lord, have I been disappointed in my prayer to you.
> *Maryam 19:4*

smiled at Sayyadna Hassan and Sayyadna Hussein and then affectionately kissed each of them on their cheeks.

That day, the people learned a very valuable lesson. Sometimes when the Prophet Muhammad ﷺ prostrated, the other children would climb on his back, when he got up from the prostration he would gently put them on the ground and they would get on his back again, and they would continue to play like this until the end of the prayer…" She smiled, "Your grandfather also knows this story, it is one of his favourites. I think he will be delighted to see his favourite grandchildren." And she lightly pushed the twins to the direction of the door.

Hamza and A'isha rushed back into the men's room and this time walked boldly up to their grandfather.

"Assalamualykum Grandpa," They said in unison. "WalaikumAssalam, what a surprise to see you here today!" Grandfather introduced them to his friends and Imam and they greeted each of their elders. A'isha passed on grandma's message and they said Salaam to everyone and walked out of the mosque holding Grandfather's hands.

Grandfather said, "Hamza, A'isha, do you know that one day the Prophet was giving a sermon and he had begun to address the huge crowd when his little grandchildren Sayyadna Hassan and Sayyadna Hussein came running over to him. They were both wearing identical red long garments which were too long for them. They kept tripping over themselves and getting up again, all the way to the front of the crowd. The Prophet came down from the pulpit, and picked them up and carried them on to the pulpit and continued with his sermon! This showed the people that you should love your children but at the same time carry on with your duties towards Allah. The Prophet was a very good grandfather."

A'isha looked up at him adoringly, "Grandpa, you are a very good grandfather too!" and Hamza nodded his head. Grandfather turned a little pink and smiled at his grandchildren and said. "And you are very good grandchildren."

They walked out of the mosque holding Grandfather's hands and soon found grandmother and together, they walked to the car park, big hand in small.

The Last Messenger

Umema Imran

One Saturday afternoon, Fatima was busy helping her Mum cook lunch. Mum would ask her to stir the pot, or peel some cucumbers, while she took care of the harder tasks. A'isha and Hamza were upstairs playing, and Ali was with them as well. Dad was out. Fatima was just taking out the dishes when Ali's cries rang through the house. Startled, Fatima put the dishes on the counter and ran upstairs to check on her baby brother. When she got there, she found him sitting near the bookshelves with books piled on top of him. A'isha and Hamza were trying to get him to stop crying. "What happened?" Fatima asked, lifting Ali in her arms and trying to console him.

"Well... we were playing catch," Hamza said hesitantly, "and I accidently threw the ball on to the book shelf and Ali was standing next to it and the books fell on him. I'm sorry."

"Okay, but be careful around Ali. He's just a baby." Fatima told him and attempted to calm Ali, but he went on bawling. Fatima was really glad when Mum came up and took her little brother from her; Ali stopped sobbing once in Mums' arm.

Ali became more relaxed as Mum rocked him and Fatima and Hamza played with him to distract him. A'isha came into the room slowly, an open book in her hands. "Hey Mum," said Fatima thoughtfully, "What's the Last Sermon?"

"The Last Sermon?" asked Mum, wondering why A'isha was asking her this question out of the blue.

"Yeah. This book fell and opened, and the title of the page said the 'Last Sermon', so I wondered." A'isha showed her Mum the book in her hands. "Hmm..." Mum said, thinking carefully, "The Last Sermon was a speech, given by the Prophet in 10 A.H. The Prophet went on a Hajj called the

The Last Sermon

In the 10th Hijri the Prophet Muhammad ﷺ went on the Hajj pilgrimage, which is known as the Farewell Hajj. He stood on a mountain to deliver his sermon then the very last verse of the Quran was revealed. Which mountain was this?

a. Arafat
b. Tur
c. Sinai

Answer: a

Hadith

The key to Paradise is prayer and the key to prayer is purification.

Ahmad

"Hajjatul-Wida.", since it would be the last hajj of his life. "Right. So on the 9th day of Dhul-Hajja, in the valley of Arafat, which is one of the places Muslims must visit during Hajj, the Prophet delivered his last sermon," Mum said.

"What did he say in the sermon?" A'isha asked.

Mum said, pulling the book on to her lap:

'O people, listen to me carefully, for I do not know whether after this year, I shall ever be amongst you again and take these words to those who could not be present here today.'

Fatima, A'isha, Hamza and even little Ali were listening attentively, hanging on to Mum's every word. "O people, just as you regard this month, this day, this city as Sacred, so regard the life and property of every one as a sacred trust. Return the goods entrusted to you to their rightful owners. Hurt no one so that no one may hurt you. Remember that you will indeed meet your Lord, and that He will indeed reckon your deeds.' Do you understand that?" Mum looked up from the book at her kids.

Fatima nodded while the twins looked uncertain. "The Prophet told the people to always return what someone gave you to keep safe and not to hurt anyone so that there would be no reason for anyone to hurt you. As a result, there is peace and no violence. He also said that whatever you do in this world, there will be a reward for good deeds and punishment for bad deeds in the hereafter. Does that help?" The twins nodded and Mum continued, "Beware of Satan, for the safety of your religion. He has lost all hope that he will be able to lead you astray in big things, so beware of following him in small things." Satan knows that good Muslims will never stop believing in Allah, but they can make mistakes. He will try to make you behave rudely, tell lies, hurt others without you realizing that it is a bad thing, so the Prophet told us to be careful about that and avoid even the small sins."

Mum read the part where the Prophet emphasized the rights of women. "Umm...what?" A'isha was confused and said to her Mum, "I don't understand this part." "The Prophet told his companions and all the Muslims to treat their wives and all women with respect and give them their rights. At the same time, he told the women to give men their rights. It creates balance in this

world. Otherwise, the world would become one-sided and unfair, and we know that Allah is not unfair. Do you understand?"

Fatima nodded, so Mum continued reading.

"O people, listen to me in earnest, worship Allah, say your five daily prayers (Salat), fast during the month of Ramadan, and give your wealth in Zakat. Perform Hajj if you can afford to."

"Wait, aren't those the five pillars of Islam?" A'isha asked.

"Yes. These are the five basic things every Muslim should do," Mum answered.

"All mankind is from Adam and Eve," Mum continued reading on, "'An Arab has no superiority over a non-Arab, nor does a non-Arab have any superiority over an Arab; also a white man has no superiority over a black man, nor does a black man have any superiority over a white man, except by piety and good actions. Learn that every Muslim is a brother to every Muslim and that the Muslims constitute one brotherhood. Nothing shall be legitimate to a Muslim, which belongs to a fellow Muslim, unless it was given freely and willingly. Do not, therefore, do injustice to yourself.' The Prophet made it clear that a person's looks and race did not make them superior to others. What makes a person better than others is the way in which he behaves. It is very wrong to judge people because of their skin colours. Allah made us all the way we are and we shouldn't make fun of anyone. The Prophet made it very clear that Allah made us all equal.

"O people, no Prophet or apostle will come after me and no new faith will be born. Reason well, therefore, O people, and understand the words, which I convey to you. I leave behind me two things, the Quran and my example and the Sunnah and, if you follow them, you will never go astray.'"

"This is a very important part," said Mum, looking seriously at her children, "It tells us that there will be no other Prophet after Prophet Muhammad ﷺ. He was the last Prophet to come into this world. Allah's message was sent to him, and he spread it throughout the land. After this Prophet, we learn

The Prophet Muhammad Passes Away

A few months after the farewell pilgrimage, Prophet Muhammad ﷺ fell ill with fever, headache and weakness. He died in Madinah, at the age of 62, in the house of his beloved wife Aisha. With his head resting on Aisha's lap, he asked her to dispose of his last worldly goods (seven coins), then murmured his final words:

When God's help and victory come, and you see people entering God's religion in multitudes, then glorify your Lord with His praise and seek His forgiveness. He is always ready to accept repentance.

Al-Nasr 110:1-3

from what he left behind for our guidance: the Quran and the Sunnah, which is a complete guide on how to live in this world. In the end part, the Prophet put emphasis upon the duty of all Muslims to spread the message of Islam."

"That's all of it?" Fatima asked.

"That's pretty much most of it," Mum shrugged, "Now tell me what you understand by all of that."

"That Muslims are supposed to believe in Allah, pray five times a day, fast, give Zakat and go for Hajj," Hamza said excitedly.

"And that Satan will make us do small sins because we won't commit big sins, so we have to be careful about that." said A'isha, "Oh, and we aren't supposed to say someone is bad because they look different or are from somewhere else…"

"and people are good because of what they do." Hamza finished his twin's sentence.

"Also, that we should follow the Quran and Sunnah, and spread the message of the Prophet." said Fatima.

"Good!" said Mum happily, "I am happy that you have learnt a lot about the life of our beloved Prophet Muhammad ﷺ. As young Muslims, you should try to find out as much as you can about our Prophet's life so that you can mould your lives accordingly. As you have learnt, the teachings of the Prophet Muhammad ﷺ show us that being a good Muslim means being a good human being. Insha'Allah, you should strive to be like the Prophet Muhammad ﷺ as much as you can, as this is an achievable goal; we can all improve ourselves, one step at a time."

Lessons from the Farewell Khutbah

"O people! Lend me an attentive ear, for I don't know whether, after this year, I shall ever be amongst you again..."

- The life and property of everyone is a sacred trust
- Hurt no one so that no one may hurt you
- Take full accountability for actions and Allah will also hold you accountable.
- Dealing with interest and usury is prohibited
- Be careful of obeying Satan in small matters
- Men have rights over women and women have rights over men
- Treat women kindly, they are your partners and committed helpers
- Women must guard their modesty and chastity
- Worship Allah by performing the prescribed prayer, fasting in Ramadan, giving charity, and performing hajj
- Muslims are brothers to one another
- Superiority of one over another is only by piety and good action, not race or colour.
- No new prophet or religion will come after this
- Follow the Quran and Sunnah and you will never go astray
- It is now your duty to pass on this message to the rest of humanity